THE CANNABIS COOKBOOK

THE
CANNABIS
COOKBOOK

OVER 35 RECIPES FOR MEALS, MUNCHIES, AND MORE

Tim Pilcher

RUNNING PRESS

FOR RED

9 8

Digit on the right indicates the number of this printing

Library of Congress Control Number: 2006939047

ISBN 10: 0-7624-3090-7
ISBN 13: 978-0-7624-3090-1

This book was created by

Ivy Press

210 High Street, Lewes,
East Sussex BN7 2NS, U.K.

CREATIVE DIRECTOR Peter Bridgewater
PUBLISHER Jason Hook
EDITORIAL DIRECTOR Caroline Earle
SENIOR PROJECT EDITOR Hazel Songhurst
ART DIRECTOR Sarah Howerd
DESIGNER Clare Barber
PHOTOGRAPHER Andrew Perris
FOOD ECONOMIST Colin Capon
PICTURE RESEARCHER Katie Greenwood
ILLUSTRATOR John Woodcock

PUBLISHER'S NOTE
We take great care to ensure that the information included in this book
is accurate and presented in good faith, but no warranty is provided nor results
guaranteed. This material is intended for informational and entertainment
purposes only. The publisher does not condone illegal activity of any kind.

This book may be ordered by mail from the publisher.
Please include $2.50 for postage and handling. But try your bookstore first!

Running Press Book Publishers
2300 Chestnut Street
Philadelphia, Pennsylvania 19103-4371
Visit us on the web!
www.runningpress.com

Contents

FOREWORD

A Chinese treatise on pharmacology attributed to Emperor Shen Nung (2737 BCE) is the earliest mention of cannabis used as an oral medicine. The Chinese diet is intimately interwoven with medicine, and recipes including cannabis soon followed. References to the oral consumption of cannabis were also made during the second millennium BCE in India (in the sacred Hindu text, *Atharva Veda*) and around 650 BCE in Assyria, as evidenced by tablets taken from the Royal Library of Ashurbanipal.

Cannabis is a nutritious fiber, and its seed a source of edible oil. As thoroughly documented throughout the ages, cannabis boasts a host of therapeutic benefits for body and mind.

(Queen Victoria's first experience of the effects of cannabis was the disappearing of her nervous headache.) Cannabis is well known for its ability to increase appetite, producing the state known as the "munchies." It is also capable of decreasing hunger and is used by various tribes in the Himalayan Mountains as an aid to religious fasting.

The effects of eating cannabis are less pronounced during the initial stages than are those of smoking it, but become significantly greater after about 20 minutes. Ingested cannabis is often more hallucinogenic than the smoke, as THC, one of the active chemicals in cannabis, is more efficiently assimilated if it has been dissolved in fats or alcohol. The presence of sugar in alcohol or in an oil-based confection facilitates the assimilation of the THC. Too much sugar, however, can interfere with the digestion of the fats and their payload of THC.

Cannabis is often mixed with tobacco and smoked, giving rise to the only rational opposition to its use: the resulting smoking mixture is likely to be carcinogenic. Cooking with cannabis neutralizes that objection, but there are many who find something unacceptably non-macho about passing around a cookie, or even a plate of cookies. Thanks to several centuries' experience of imbibing alcohol, drinking a cannabis potion suffers from no such hostility. Recipes for cannabis drinks are rare, but you'll find a few in here, including one from my old friend, Sam Peacefull-Day, straight from the exquisite Eric's Kitchen. You'll also find a recipe from me. Enjoy.

Howard Marks, November 2006

INTRODUCTION

While there have been many books on cooking with cannabis throughout history, most notably Alice B. Toklas's classic collection of recipes (this wise old bird was the Betty Crocker of cannabis catering), the time has never been riper for a fresh approach. With tobacco smoking on the decline, and bars, restaurants, and other public places banning the practice anyway, the old-school method of getting high is becoming passé. People are turning away from the tradition of sharing a joint (which was very often mixed with tobacco) but are still looking for that nice, warm, glowing, giggly feeling that only comes from cannabis. What better way to sample the most popular weed on the planet than by eating it, as people have done for thousands of years?

CANNABIS FOR THE THIRD AGE

This book examines the history of cannabis in the kitchen from ancient Scythians to latter-day pioneer chefs. Cooking with cannabis has never been more popular, not only with the "stoner generations" but increasingly with older people. These ganja grannies and grandpas are

Cannabis Sativa wasn't classified until 1753 when botanist Carolus Linnaeus listed it as a monotypic species, a sole specimen of its genus.

cooking up treats for family and friends not to get high but for more important reasons. The ethical and moral battle for the right to medical marijuana continues to rage, but in the meantime a quiet revolution is taking place in the kitchens of ordinary people who are making delicious stews and casseroles full of grass to ease the pain of chronic arthritis and multiple sclerosis. Technically they're criminals, but is it wrong when the only way they can ease their suffering is by making criminally delicious, dope-laden delights?

Great grass recipes don't have to be too complex—sometimes less is more, such as this ganja-filled guacamole.

BEYOND COOKIES

This book includes a selection of classic recipes, some old favorites and some new twists. Most importantly it should be noted that all these recipes are equally delicious with or without that "secret ingredient." This cookbook is not about simply sticking a few leaves in a salad, or crumbling some hash on top of a sandwich, it's about cooking, and all the joy

and passion that comes with it. All the recipes are very easy to make and needn't daunt the novice. There are a few that don't even involve cooking, such as the Grassy Knoll Guacamole (*see page 34*), so there's no chance of burning your lungs or your fingers. Wherever possible, shortcuts are suggested in the recipe methods, to make life easier without compromising any of the quality and flavor of the end results.

🌿 *Cooking with cannabis can take many forms and includes both sweet and savory dishes. This delicious "Freaky Fridge Cake" is a perfect munchie treat.*

CANNABIS DINNER PARTIES

Cannabis cooking can be incredibly diverse. A popular misconception among the uninitiated is that the only "meals" that can be made with cannabis are sweet, baked foods like "Space Cake," "Hash Brownies," and "Cannabis Cookies." While these all have their place, and are undeniably delicious if cooked well, it is in fact possible to create an entire dinner party—from aperitifs and appetizers to desserts and coffee—using the cannabis recipes in this book. Should you plan a banquet of this kind, however, make sure to include only extremely small quantities of cannabis in each dish, as the effect is cumulative

BE PREPARED

Getting the essential groundwork out of the way in advance will allow you to prepare the recipes that much faster when you want to chill out. You can follow the step-by-step instructions in this book to build supplies of ghee, cannabutter, and tinctures, to form the basis of your cooking.

and you don't want to send your dinner guests reeling into the night, or knock them out completely!

CELEBRITY RECIPES

Also included are original recipes from some of the leading lights of the world of wacky weed. These all-around proponents of pot include authors, artists, and campaigners, who have each contributed their favorite way of savoring sinsemilla without smoking.

HEMP

Hemp is so diverse that you can eat it and make it into soap.

The recipes don't stop at food. This green gastronomic tome goes beyond the conventional cookbook to show you how to utilize hemp in everyday products, such as a soothing hemp massage oil. Plus there's advice and recipes on how to make your own hemp seed soap and fizzing bath bomb—all from the very same plant you're cooking up for dinner. So let's get busy in the kitchen—it's guaranteed you'll be taking it easy later!

THE HISTORY OF CANNABIS IN THE KITCHEN

It's doubtful that there is another plant on this planet as versatile as cannabis when it comes to cooking. Every single part of the plant is edible, including the leaves, buds, seeds, and even the stalks. It can be served in endless ways: raw in a salad, sprinkled over casseroles, or ground down to make hemp flour for pasta and bread.

Cannabis's illustrious culinary chronicles date far back into the mists of time. Some believe that the innocent eating of the hempen plant of pleasure—in the Eden-like forests of the ancient world—gave rise to the notion of a god to primitive *Homo sapiens*. Forbidden fruit indeed. Professor Richard E. Schultz, Director of the Botanical Museum at the University of Harvard, and a prominent researcher of psychoactive plants, comments, "Upon eating hemp, the euphoric, ecstatic, and hallucinatory aspects may have introduced man to an other-worldly plane from which emerged religious beliefs, perhaps even the concept of a deity. The plant becomes accepted as a special gift of the gods, a sacred medium for communication with the spiritual world and as such it has remained in some cultures to the present." Food of the gods, indeed.

Fabric and Food

As early as 3000 BCE the Chinese were weaving fabric from hemp and were eating the seeds, and up until 500 BCE farmers grew this "pseudo cereal" as part of their staple diet, alongside rice, barley, millet, and soybeans. Often the seeds were roasted whole, ground into meal, or cooked down into oatmeal. This meant that they could have made anything from unleven bread to noodles, using hemp flour.

MYSTIC FOODSTUFF

Throughout history, cannabis has also acquired medical, religious, and mythical status. In Indian mythology it's believed that the deity Shiva was the first being to eat cannabis leaves. Shiva adopted the plant as his favorite food, thus gaining the title, Lord of Bhang (*bhanga* is Sanskrit for hemp). Even today Saduhs, or holy men, chew the leaves for their mild sedative effect in honor of their god, in the same way that coca leaves are used habitually in South America. It's also believed that the Buddha survived for six years on a single hemp seed a day. The Indian sub-continent also gave birth to one of the more well-known cannabis beverages, also called Bhang. This heady brew of milk or yogurt, marijuana, almonds, and spices is

The Roman physician Galen, originally from Greece, knew the benefits of cannabis.

Hindu god Shiva makes the traditional Indian drink of Bhang using a pestle and mortar to mash up the cannabis leaves and milk.

such an integral part of Indian life that it is looked upon as the traditional relaxant, in the way that a beer is enjoyed after a hard day's work in the West.

BENEFICIAL HERB

The Greek philosopher Democritus (460–370 BCE) stated that cannabis was drunk with wine and myrrh to create states for visions, and later the medicinal uses of cannabis were also discovered, when the 2nd-century CE Chinese surgeon Hua T'o created an anesthetic using wine and hemp seeds. Around the same time, the Roman physician Galen (129–199 CE) noted that rich Roman gourmets served a cannabis-seed dessert, which had widely beneficial effects, although he also observed that over-indulgence led to dehydration and impotence in men.

🌿 *16th-century whirling dervishes from the mystical Islamic sect, the Sufis.*

Galen's own recipe of chopped dried seeds, sifted and mixed with water and filtered through muslin, was possibly intended to be drunk as an analgesic. Because they were prevented from drinking alcohol by the teachings of the Koran—but were still allowed to partake of cannabis—around the eleventh century, Arabs in the Middle East developed hashish-based sweets known as *mahjoun*, made from cannabis, dried fruit, nuts, and honey mashed into a sticky paste. These delicious confections

became particularly popular in Egypt and Morocco. The 13th-century Sufis of the Middle East also adopted cannabis as a sacrament, developing a dope-laden "chewing gum" to aid their whirling dervishes and contact with God.

Elsewhere in the world cannabis has been perennially prepared for repasts. Even today, in remote regions such as Nepal, hemp oil and seeds are used regularly in cooking. While in Poland and Lithuania, in the late 1950s renowned Polish anthropologist, Sula Benet, rediscovered an old traditional dish "Semieniatka," a soup made from crushed cannabis seeds. This was traditionally served on Christmas Eve, and in Latvia and the Ukraine on Three Kings' Day (January 6).

HASH EATERS

In 1844 Paris, Dr. Jacques-Joseph Moreau and renowned author Théophile Gautier formed the infamous Club des Hashichins (The Hash Eaters' Club). The group, active for about five years, was dedicated to the exploration of drug-induced experiences, notably with hashish. Members included such literary luminaries as Charles Baudelaire, Gérard de Nerval, Eugène Delacroix, and Alexandre Dumas. Dr. Moreau would often administer a "green paste" of hash for members, mixed in with strong Arabic coffee, called dawamesk. Other ingredients included hashish, cinnamon, cloves, nutmeg, pistachio, sugar, orange juice, butter, and extract of beetle, or "Spanish Fly" as it was otherwise known.

Alexandre Dumas

Alexandre Dumas, a member of the Club des Hashichins, wrote about hashish in many of his stories, including his 1844 classic, *The Count of Monte Cristo*: "When you return to this mundane sphere from your visionary world, you would seem to leave a Neapolitan spring for a Lapland winter—to quit paradise for earth—heaven for hell! Taste the hashish, guest of mine—taste the hashish!"

THE COUNT OF MONTE CRISTO

ALEXANDRE DUMAS

CONTEMPORARY COOKS

More recent times have seen a big resurgence in cannabis cooking, kick-started by the now legendary Alice B. Toklas. Toklas was Gertrude Stein's lover, secretary, muse, editor, and significantly, also her cook. After Stein died in 1946, Toklas published her memoir, a mixture of reminiscences and recipes under the title *The Alice B. Toklas Cookbook*. It included a recipe given by her friend Brion Gysin called "Hashisch Fudge," a mixture of fruit, nuts, spices, and "canibus sativa" [sic]. The cookbook was a huge success and has barely been out of print since it was published.

Name Game

The success of Toklas's cookbook led to a range of cannabis concoctions named "Alice B. Toklas Brownies." Her reputation was forever entwined with cannabis cookery when the eponymous 1965 movie *I Love You, Alice B. Toklas* was released. In the movie Peter Sellers plays a straight-laced lawyer who discovers the joys of cooking with the sacred herb.

Alice B. Toklas (right) and her lover Gertrude Stein try to remember if they left the stove on.

MARIJUANA AS MEDICINE

The modern era of medicinal marijuana—as a serious herbal/homeopathic cure for numerous symptoms arising from a wide range of medical conditions, including asthma and multiple sclerosis—has seen a sharp rise in people wishing to consume cannabis orally. The pain relief, and other benefits, that cannabis can bring has meant that many people have been prosecuted for producing dope-laden dinners that were intended only to relieve suffering.

One such case was Patricia Tabram, a 66-year-old British grandmother who was arrested in 2004 for supplying sinsemilla stews, pot pies, and other cannabis meals to her arthritic friends. Her court case has highlighted the prevalence of cannabis cooking among the general public, while bringing to attention the archaic current anti-marijuana laws. Tabram continues to cook with the "holy herb" and to be harassed by the British police. She hopes to write her own recipe book, *Grandma Eats Cannabis*, which will include her experiences with the law, as well as campaigning for support for the right to self-medicate with marijuana.

Despite the negativity of a few ill-informed individuals, cannabis cooking today is thriving. After all, you are far less likely to be arrested in possession of a cake than a joint.

And the final word has to go to the legendary painter Salvador Dali who said, "Everyone should eat hashish, but only once."

The Netherlands was the first country to legalize and facilitate medical marijuana. Physicians, hospitals, and pharmacies can prescribe various doses to patients that come either as dried marijuana flowers, in tea, or turned into a tincture for spraying in a nebulizer.

The Basics

A careful cook understands the changeable nature of his or her ingredients. Cannabis, like any other natural food, will change its properties according to the cooking process. The information given in this chapter will help you prepare it right, so your creations have optimum effectiveness.

The cannabis plant has three strains—*Cannabis sativa*, *Cannabis indica*, and *Cannabis ruderalis*—and all contain some THC, the psychoactive element that is released when either smoked, or better, heated in a cooking process.

Cannabis ruderalis (known as "industrial hemp") contains only minute traces of THC, but most cannabis grown for recreational use (*Cannabis sativa* and *Cannabis indica*) contains much more THC, with some plants made up of a mind-blowing 25 percent. *Cannabis sativa* is far more likely to be known by its strain or "street" name, such as Kushman's Kush, White Widow, or the tremendously popular—and powerful—Skunk. Each strain has been grown to produce various types of highs, from giggly and uplifting, to mellow, if not downright soporific, so this chapter also covers the science and "ground rules" every ganja gastronaut needs to know before embarking on a culinary cannabis adventure.

THE SCIENCE OF COOKING WITH CANNABIS

It's the female cannabis plant's sweet resin that connoisseurs crave. The male plant is taller, skinnier, and has flower-like pods, which contain the fertilizing pollen-generating anthers. The female plant is darker, shorter, and generally squatter. Cannabis is quite hardy, and can survive in most conditions (it's not called "weed" for nothing!).

DELTA 9-TETRAHYDRACANNABINOL (THC)

The trichomes are the fronds on the tips of the plant that are the holy grail of hash cooking. They are found on the tips of the sweetest buds.

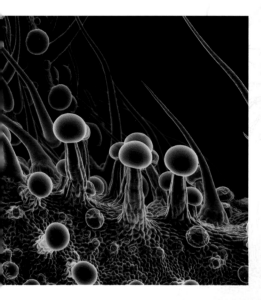

Cannabis is the only plant known to contain the chemical elements cannabinoids. More than 60 cannabinoids have been discovered and isolated, but only six of them are psychoactive and give that beloved buzz. The most well known is Delta 9-Tetrahydracannabinol, or THC.

In order to enjoy the benefits of THC, it needs to be extracted from the seeds, buds, or leaves. The sticky buds contain the highest levels of THC and the leaves the least. Unfortunately, THC is only soluble in oils and fats so it won't break down in water on its own. The best way to prepare THC for cooking is to create a supply of cannabutter or ghee (*see pages 24–26*). This can then be used in recipes as a replacement for regular butter or cooking oil.

The purest form of THC that can be extracted from cannabis is from the pollen. This can be taken from the very tips of the buds using an Ice-o-Later bag (*see* Glossary, *page 123*), which will separate the precious pollen from the less active leaf and stalk material. Pollen, like all precious herbs and spices, should be added to the cooking process at the last possible moment. The remaining leaves and stalks needn't be wasted, but can be put into an electric grinder or blender to produce a fine powder for use in other recipes. Breaking the plant down in this way will help to release its THC content.

Quality buds are the best part of the plant to cook with as they contain the highest levels of THC.

Gently Does It

While extremely high temperatures or overcooking can destroy THC activity, careful cooking can increase potency by activating otherwise dormant THC. The trick is to experiment and play around with cooking times and temperatures, but it's always best to cook for longer on a medium heat than to blast the food and to cook it too quickly. Nice and easy does it!

HIGHS AND LOWS

The high that you experience from cannabis varies according to which psychoactive cannabinoids are coming into play. For example, Cannabidiol, or CBD, appears in most forms of cannabis in varying degrees, and lends a sedative effect to the high experience. CBD has the tendency to delay, but also prolong, the high. Whether CBD increases or decreases the strength of the high depends on the individual's tolerance. Cannabinol, or CBN, is produced as THC oxidizes or degrades. Only trace amounts appear in fresh buds, but stored or cured (dried) buds and hashish tend to have higher amounts of CBN because the THC has degraded in the preparation process. Research has revealed that CBN gives a smoker a disoriented or sleepy effect, known as a "stupefying high"—perfect for cooking. The compound associated with the fragrance of the plant is THCV, or Tetrahydrocannabivarin, and pungent smelling cannabis, like Skunk, usually contains high amounts of THCV. These high concentrations of THCV will make the high come on quicker, but last a shorter time. Ultimately it's all down to personal choice. Knowing which strain is used, and its effects, will enhance any cannabis chef's culinary capabilities.

The brain is magically in tune to receive cannabis THC thanks to unique receptors such as anandamide, whose name comes from ananda, *the Sanskrit word for bliss.*

COOKING WITH CANNABIS: IMPORTANT FACTS

Its medicinal impact notwithstanding, cooking with cannabis is probably better described as an art than a science. There is no definitive recipe that will hit exactly the right spot for everyone. A little trial and error is required to establish exactly how much cannabis, and in what form it should be added to a meal to maximize the enjoyment of your guests.

EATING VS. SMOKING

There are some key facts that every cannabis connoisseur must be aware of before preparing gastronomic ganja. Firstly, eating cannabis is a completely different experience from smoking it, in several ways. When smoking a joint, users often get an instant rush or hit from the first toke. Others may get progressively more stoned over the period of hits, but the effects are still pretty much instantaneous. Eating the plant is a much slower process, and diners may not feel any peak highs for anything up to two hours after consuming it. Marijuana's effect is also intensified when eaten, meaning less is required to get the same high as a joint. Finally, the effects last a lot longer—anything up to five to six hours—which makes a cannabis-laden dish the perfect centerpiece of an evening dinner party from which no one has to rush off afterward!

> **LESS IS MORE**
>
> Generally speaking, when sampling cannabis cookery it is safer to err on the side of caution. Less can be more, as the author found out to his cost on one memorable (or not so memorable) occasion when the entire dinner party passed out for 12 hours!

Cannabis goes well with practically any food, from traditional "Hash Brownies" to more unusual pasta dishes.

One day these seedlings will grow up to blow the minds of appreciative gastronauts.

FOOTPRINT AWARENESS

Eating or drinking cannabis can be risky, due to the possible presence of contaminants and/or pathogens, and if your grass comes from a sprayed crop you can be sure you're ingesting things that your body won't appreciate. The U.S. government regularly sprays crops in producer countries with cancer-causing herbicides. Cooking at a high temperature will kill most pathogens, but maybe not all of them—and if the oven is cranked up too high the THC will be destroyed.

As you would with any "traditional" ingredient, it makes sense to know the "footprint" history of your cannabis. Try to find a reliable grower whose crop is organic and can be visited. Ideally it will be grown alongside rosemary, thyme, basil, and other herbs. Alternatively, to ensure a constant supply, cannabis can be grown—it is a hardy plant and very easy to propagate. Seeds can be ordered legally off the Internet.

A WORD TO THE WISE

As with all cooking ingredients, you get what you pay for. There are unscrupulous people out there selling strains such as Skunk with insanely high levels of THC, or low-grade hashish known as Soap Bar (which can contain anything from engine oil to feces). At the very least, never eat street cannabis that hasn't been cooked, for example, hash that has just been crumbled up and sprinkled on a salad. You might get off lightly with a bad stomach and the runs—but you could conceivably end up with hepatitis.

Cannabis can be served in two forms of liquid—tinctures and the more potent hash oil.

> **WARNING**
> Note that excessive oral consumption of cannabis in any form, be it in food or tinctures, can have nasty short-term psychological side effects, such as panic attacks, and may spark dormant longer-term issues such as paranoid schizophrenia.

MAKING CANNABIS GHEE AND CANNABUTTER

Almost every recipe in this book uses either cannabutter or cannabis ghee as the means of integrating active THC into quality food. There are many different ways to prepare these, but the methods given here can be followed for all the recipes.

Ghee

Ghee, or "sacred ghee," as the Hindus call it, is clarified butter and is often used in Indian recipes. It is also a great facilitator of THC extraction because the fats link on to the THC molecules and make absorption more effective. Properly prepared ghee can be kept at room temperature or in a moderately cool place for many months without spoiling. You can buy it ready-made from specialist shops, or make it yourself, as follows:

Ingredients
2lb/1–1.5kg unsalted butter

METHOD 1

The unsalted butter is heated in a pan at a medium–low temperature (hot enough to boil the butter). A froth will form on the surface, which should be skimmed off with a spoon. This is repeated until no more froth appears. The remaining butterfat is ghee, best stored in a refrigerator.

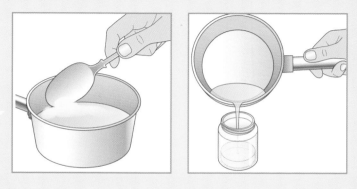

Ghee

METHOD 2

1 2lb/1kg unsalted butter is melted in a wok at medium–low temperature and allowed to simmer for a while. White particles will float to the top. The melted butter should be stirred frequently to ensure that nothing sticks to the bottom.

2 Eventually the butter will start to bubble over, so the wok should be removed from the stove and allowed to stand for about 5 minutes, while the white particles sink to the bottom. When they have settled the ghee is poured into a jar.

3 For purer ghee, the liquid is filtered through several layers of cheesecloth while hot. This reduces its butterscotch flavor. The color of the ghee should be slightly darker than gold. If it is any darker the wok was too hot.

4 Once cooled, the ghee can be used in any recipe requiring margarine or butter. The residue can also be eaten and enjoyed, with honey, for example.

Cannabis Ghee

The next stage is to add the special ingredient. Getting the strength right is difficult, as this depends on the quantity and strength of the cannabis. A ratio of around 1oz/28g cannabis to 1lb/500g of ghee is recommended. Care should be taken when melting the ghee as, being free from impurities, it can get very hot very quickly.

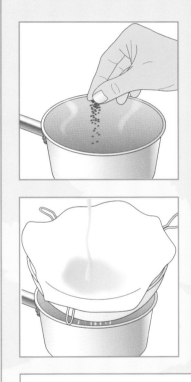

METHOD

1 The ghee is melted and allowed to simmer, so that the oil is not burning or cooling off.

2 The crumbled/powdered cannabis is sprinkled in and stirred gently. It is heated and stirred occasionally for approximately 1 hour, until the THC fully dissolves.

3 Once the ghee is cooked, a clean cloth is placed in a strainer and the hot mixture drained into a pan or bowl, then allowed to cool.

USING GHEE

To make a batch of cannabis cakes or cookies a ratio of $\frac{1}{16}$ oz/2g to 10 cookies is a good way to start. The cookies can be eaten one at a time, as required.

Cannabutter

Similar to ghee, cannabutter is actually better for cooking sweet dishes such as cookies and cakes. It should be noted, however, that the butter will burn at a lower temperature than ghee, so extra care needs to be taken.

Ingredients

1–2lb/0.5–1kg butter or ghee

2–3oz/55–85g of finely ground/ powdered cannabis*

*see pages 28–29 for specific requirements

METHOD 1

1 The butter is melted in a pan and several ounces of the powdered cannabis added. It is simmered and stirred for a few minutes until the butter turns a greenish color.

2 The butter is then strained through a very fine strainer, and remaining leafy material retained.

3 To really crank up the wow factor, step 1 can be repeated by heating fresh cannabis in the same butter.

4 When cool it can be frozen or refrigerated until required but water should be poured over it first to stop air getting to it. Cannabutter can be kept for a long time in this way.

5 The left-over leafy material can be simmered in hot milk or vodka and sweetened with honey to make a tasty and powerful drink. Or it can be used in one of the recipes in this book.

METHOD 2

1 ¼ cup/30g crushed and crumbled marijuana tops are added to a pan and the rest filled with a mixture of 1 part butter and 4—or more—parts water. It is boiled for 30 minutes, stirring frequently.

2 As much debris from the bottom of the pan as possible is removed. The liquids should cool to room temperature, then be refrigerated. The butter will harden on the top and can be removed. The water is discarded.

3 If a stronger butter is required, step 1 is repeated with fresh water and grass.

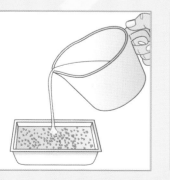

ALTERNATIVE

Hashish or hash oil can be used for a potent cannabutter. It is heated and stirred until the hash or oil dissolves in the butter.

TINCTURES

THC, the main psychoactive chemical of cannabis, breaks down well in fats and oils, but it is also soluble in alcohol so a variety of cannabis drinks can be made.

Basic Tincture

One way to make a drinkable form of cannabis is to infuse it in a strong spirit to create a tincture (marijuana in liquid form). Tinctures tend to taste bitter so a reasonably sweet drink with a high percentage of alcohol is recommended, such as a fruit schnapps. Try 1 part cannabis to 3–5 parts alcohol, or follow the recipe below:

Ingredients:

¾oz/22g marijuana leaves and/or flowers (or resin, if that's all you have)

3fl oz/90ml alcohol (brandy, flavored schnapps or similar—40 to 70% proof minimum)

METHOD

1 The cannabis is ground down to make a powder. Grass is better than resin because it tends to be purer, and therefore it is easier to filter out the solid bits that remain after extraction.

2 The cannabis powder is soaked overnight in warm water. This removes any water-soluble impurities but not any of that precious THC.

3 The excess water is drained off and the cannabis placed in an airtight jar. The alcohol is poured over.

4 The mixture is kept in a cool, dark place for about 10 days and shaken daily. Then it is filtered through a strainer or, if resin has been used, a coffee filter, to avoid the, now inert, bits getting into the final drink. The filtering process should be repeated at least once—the more it is filtered, the more the tincture will be improved and strengthened.

5 The green/brown colored tincture should be stored somewhere dark and cold. Most of the THC will have been absorbed within a week, but connoisseurs tend to leave it for a year or more.

6 The cannabis tincture can be enjoyed neat or dissolved in a drink or in food.

WEIGHTS AND MEASURES

When it comes to working out specific amounts for recipes, cannabis can be a tricky customer. What may create a fantastic buzz for one diner is likely to freak out another. But there are ways of gauging it.

When cooking with cannabis the hardest aspect to control and get right is the quantity of grass you should add to any given recipe. The balance can be tipped completely depending on the strength of the strain, the intensity of the cannabutter or ghee, and the quantity of other ingredients (the last two aspects are in the control of the cook, but the strain isn't). One good rule of thumb is to use slightly more than the combined amount each person would smoke in a single session (spread over however many dishes you are preparing). Always begin small and slowly work up. Too many people have eaten too much too soon and regretted it later.

Recreational Use

Suggested amount of cannabis for recreational use per person

WEIGHT OF PERSON	AMOUNT OF CANNABIS BUD PER PERSON PER MEAL
Under 126lb (57kg)	¼–⅓ teaspoon
126–182lb (57–83kg)	½–⅔ teaspoon
182–224lb (83–102kg)	⅔–1 teaspoon
224–280lb (102–128kg)	1–1½ teaspoons
294lbs+ (134kg+)	1½–2 teaspoons

HIGH NOTES

Once you've found your happy high, either by eating more of your meal or experimenting with quantities of the key ingredient, you might want to note down your findings to refer back to later—if a pad and paper can be found that is. If the high's worth having, you won't want to rely on your memory!

RECOMMENDED DOSES FOR MEDICINAL PURPOSES

If cooking for medicinal purposes, such as for pain relief, a smaller amount is required than would be for pleasure, as the diner should be able to function normally after their meal. Assess the body weight of whoever you're treating, then use the chart below as a guide. The best way to measure quantities is to use a level teaspoon of ground cannabis powder and divide it up according to weight. Stick to the formula because overindulgence will only make the patient sleepy. However, tolerance builds up over time so you may need to up the dosage.

Cannabis taken in food is a far more effective method of pain relief than simply smoking it as the effect from a joint only lasts 90 minutes, whereas taken orally it can last for five hours.

Medicinal Use

Suggested amount of cannabis for medicinal use per person

WEIGHT OF PERSON	AMOUNT OF CANNABIS BUD PER PERSON
Under 126lb (57kg)	⅙ teaspoon
126–182lb (57–83kg)	¼ teaspoon
182–224lb (83–102kg)	⅓ teaspoon
224–280lb (102–128kg)	⅓ teaspoon
294lbs+ (134kg+)	1 level teaspoon

NOTE

If you want to get wasted, don't follow the guidelines on this chart or you'll be disappointed!

Stoned Starters

"They've outlawed the number one vegetable on the planet," bemoaned New Age guru and acid head Timothy Leary, back in the Sixties. And while it's not actually a vegetable (technically, it's a fruit), it is true that for some reason governments really have it in for this seemingly innocuous plant. Ever since its ban was introduced into America in 1937, cannabis prohibition has been one of the country's most consistently broken laws. Yet in earlier times, pot was praised—the American founding fathers were huge *Sativa* and *Indica* fans, and George Washington himself wrote, "Make the most of hemp seed. Sow it everywhere." Still, the argument has a long way to run and genuine dialog between prohibitionists and decriminalizers has only just really gotten started.

Speaking of starting, any one of the recipes in this section will set the tone for the rest of your meal—light and easy with nothing too heavy, man. They can be equally enjoyed as light snacks on their own, to help even the toughest of days float by. One of the great joys of getting stoned is indulging in the munchies.

NOTE

All the recipes featured in this book use a combination of hash resin and various parts of the natural plant (grass).

Ganja Garlic Bread

This is the perfect stoner snack as it requires absolute minimal effort! It goes perfectly with the Puffed-Up Pizza (*see page 50*) or the Chile Bean Pot (*see page 61*), a few friends, and a classic Cheech and Chong movie… "Dave? Dave's not here!" "No, man. I am Dave!"

YOU WILL NEED

1 baguette or French stick/loaf
3–5 garlic cloves, chopped
    (depends how garlicky you like it!)
handful of fresh basil leaves, chopped
roughly 11oz/300g cannabutter*
    or about an $\frac{1}{8}$ of a bud
*see pages 28–29 for specific requirements

SERVES 2–4

HOW TO PREPARE

1 The bread should be cut diagonally along the length at about 3in/7.5cm intervals, but not cut all the way through.

2 All the other ingredients can now go into a bowl and be gently mixed into a paste until there's an even spread of herbs through the butter.

3 The mix should be liberally spread in each cut in the bread and baked in a hot oven (400°F/200°C) for 20 minutes, or until all the butter has melted and the bread starts to turn brown. This tastes best straight from the oven, cut into mouthwatering slices.

SERVING SUGGESTION

The garlic bread can be cut all the way through and grated cheese sprinkled on top (mozzarella or Cheddar is good) and placed under a hot broiler until the cheese is melted.

Grassy Knoll Guacamole

It's reputed that former U.S. President John F. Kennedy was partial to the odd toke of wacky baccy to ease his back pain, so here's one for all the crazy cannabis conspiracy theorists. It works great as a dip with tortillas or chips, alongside an enchilada, or taco, or even as a side salad. It's also the perfect complement to the Stoned Spicy Salsa (*see page 37*). Guaranteed to blow your brains out.

YOU WILL NEED

1 fresh red chile

juice of 2 limes

1 tbsp extra virgin olive oil

2²/₃ tsp finely chopped or ground cannabis buds*

3 large ripe avocados

¹/₂ cup/80g very finely chopped onion

*see pages 28–29 for specific requirements

SERVES 2–4

HOW TO PREPARE

1 Everything needs to be mixed together apart from the avocados and onion and left to stand for about an hour. The lime juice will react with the rest of the ingredients to draw out the flavors and THC.

2 The avocados and onion can then be added and mashed up. A hand blender will give a really smooth mix.

3 Usually served with tacos, heated pitas, or as a dip. Guacamole is best enjoyed fresh, but this can be kept chilled, for up to three days, because the lime juice prevents the avocados from turning brown.

Stoned Spicy Salsa

Mexican salsas were traditionally produced using a *molcajete* (a kind of mortar and pestle), but nowadays we can use blenders. Well-known salsas include salsa roja, made with cooked tomatoes, onion, garlic, and fresh cilantro, salsa cruda, aka *pico de gallo* or "cock's beak," and salsa mexicana. This recipe is for salsa fresca, probably the best of them all. You can blend it smooth or leave it slightly chunky and roughly chopped.

YOU WILL NEED

1 small red onion, chopped

2 large tomatoes, seeds removed

juice of 1 lime and some grated rind

1 small fresh red chile, chopped

1 yellow bell pepper, chopped

1 green bell pepper, chopped

bunch of fresh cilantro

$\frac{1}{8}$ tsp ground or chopped premium
   cannabis bud *

see pages 28–29 for specific requirements

SERVES 2—4

HOW TO PREPARE

1 It's not complicated: it gets all mixed up in a bowl. But no tomato seeds can be allowed into the mix because they'll make the salsa soggy.

2 Salsa can be served as a refreshing side dish, or as a snack with nachos.

Green Day Salad with Marijuana Mustard Dressing

The incredibly popular rock band Green Day take their name from the slang for a particularly heavy smoking session. Hopefully this salad will do as advertised, although the leaves of the cannabis plant actually contain the least amount of THC. It makes a great light appetizer before moving on to a stronger main course.

YOU WILL NEED

Salad

2 large handfuls of arugula

handful of watercress

handful of fresh basil

2 large handfuls of baby spinach

large handful of fresh cannabis leaves*

Dressing

1 heaping tbsp Dijon mustard

5 tbsp virgin olive oil

2 tbsp balsamic vinegar

1 tsp ground cannabis bud*

salt and pepper

*see pages 28–29 for specific requirements

SERVES 4

HOW TO PREPARE

1   All the leaves need a thorough rinse, the basil should be torn, and then it can all be chucked into a large salad bowl.

2   All the dressing ingredients get mixed together in a small glass bottle (an old preserving jar is good). With the lid on tight, it's shaken like crazy.

3   The dressing is drizzled over the salad and can be served as an appetizer, or with the Pot Pesto & 'Erb Pasta (*see page 52*) or Seriously Sprouted Hemp Seed Falafels (*see page 62*).

ALTERNATIVE

As an additional garnish, sprouted hemp seeds could be added to your salad. See page 62 if this sounds interesting.

Really Wild Mushroom Sauté

This wonderful mix of mushrooms will dance on anybody's taste buds. Any range of great 'shrooms will do, but a combination of shiitake, oyster, porcini, and trompettes de mort is ideal. These babies are a delight both in the spring and fall. And yes, the magical variety of 'shroom could go in here too, for the more experienced and hardy psychonaut. Just don't make any plans for the main course or dessert.

YOU WILL NEED

3–4 garlic cloves, chopped
small handful of fresh thyme
small handful of fresh oregano
small handful of fresh rosemary
3 heaping tbsp cannabutter*
14oz/425g mixture of wild
　　mushrooms, chopped
small handful of fresh parsley
1 tbsp red wine vinegar
$\frac{1}{2}$ tsp granulated sugar
salt and pepper
lemon wedges, to serve
*see pages 28–29 for specific requirements

SERVES 4

HOW TO PREPARE

1 The garlic and all the herbs apart from the parsley are sauteéd in the melted butter for about 4 minutes.

2 The mushrooms are added, salt and pepper is added for seasoning, and then it gets left to cook for about 7 minutes.

3 Finally, the parsley, vinegar, and sugar are mixed together, poured over the mushrooms and stirred in. The meal is served with lemon wedges.

Onion & Sativa Soup

After an afternoon's walk kicking up the leaves, this heartwarming soup is perfect to mellow out with on a dusky fall evening. Simply grab a few of the best kind of "sweet leaf" and get yourself busy in the kitchen.

YOU WILL NEED

4–6 large onions, sliced

a large amount cannabutter* or ghee

4 tbsp all-purpose flour

4 cups/1 liter hot water or stock

salt and pepper

cooking brandy

salt and pepper to taste

*see pages 28–29 for specific requirements

SERVES 4

HOW TO PREPARE

1 The onions are sautéed in the cannabutter on low heat, until they're golden brown.

2 The pan is removed from the heat and the flour stirred in. The pan should be covered and left to sit on low heat for 5 minutes or so, stirring occasionally.

3 The hot water is added and sluiced over the sides of the pan, so as to incorporate the precious fats. Seasoning is added to taste.

4 It's left to simmer for 30 minutes. A little cooking brandy would give it some zip. It should be stirred really well just before serving as the oil containing the THC rises to the surface.

SERVING SUGGESTION

The soup is served out in individual bowls, then some French bread slices are laid on top of each bowl of soup, with loads of hard cheese all over (Parmesan and Cheddar are excellent). Before serving, each bowl can be popped under a hot broiler until all the cheese has melted. Delicious!

Naughty Cheese Nuggets

This is a great dish that works just as well as a snack on its own or as an appetizer. Try serving them with cranberry sauce or a raspberry coulis dip. But be warned, these nuggets can be very more-ish so pace yourself!

YOU WILL NEED

scant 1²/₃ cups/18oz/250g all-purpose flour, preferably whole wheat

4oz/115g cannabutter* or ghee

2 cups/8oz/250g grated aged Cheddar

1 tsp garam masala or cumin powder

1 large egg yolk

1 large egg white (beaten)

toasted hemp or sesame seeds, crushed

*see pages 28–29 for specific requirements

MAKES 30

HOW TO PREPARE

1 The flour and butter are mixed together, then the cheese and spice are added and mixed in too.

2 The addition of egg yolk means it can be shaped into balls, using about 2 teaspoons of the mixture for each.

3 The balls are dipped into the beaten egg white and then into the seeds until they are evenly coated.

4 The balls are baked in the oven, preheated to 375°F/190°C, on an ungreased baking sheet for 15 minutes.

SERVING SUGGESTION

A nice spicy Monterey Jack or a good quality crumbly Gruyère can be used as an alternative to Cheddar.

HOWARD MARKS'

"Green, Green Grass of Home" Fritters

Here is a recipe based on the Middle Eastern snack *mücer*, with a hint of the Welsh national emblem, the leek. The title comes from the famous song recorded by Tom Jones and Elvis Presley—two great Welshmen. Don't believe me? Then read *Señor Nice* and discover what else Wales has brought to the world.

YOU WILL NEED

2 eggs

1/2 cup/125ml plain yogurt

3 1/2 oz/100g feta cheese, crumbled

1 tsp baking powder

2 tbsp finely chopped fresh parsley

1 tbsp finely chopped fresh mint

1 tsp finely ground cannabis bud*

3 tbsp all-purpose plain flour

8oz/250g zucchini, grated

8oz/250g leeks, chopped

salt and pepper to taste

*see pages 28–29 for specific requirements

MAKES 25–30

HOW TO PREPARE

1 The eggs are beaten in a large bowl, then the yogurt, herbs, baking powder, and feta are added and mixed in.

2 The zucchini and leeks are added and mixed together.

3 Heaping teaspoons of the mix are dropped on to to an oiled baking sheet.

4 The fritters are baked in the oven, preheated to 400°F/200°C for 15 minutes and then turned over until both sides are lightly brown and crispy.

HOWARD MARKS

In the 1980s, Howard Marks owned 43 aliases, 89 phone lines, and 25 companies—all money-laundering fronts serving his core activity: dope dealing. One of the biggest cannabis smugglers in the world, Marks moved huge quantities of hashish into Europe and America concealed in the equipment of rock bands. In 1988, he was busted in a worldwide operation by the DEA and sentenced to 25 years in a U.S. prison. Released on parole in 1995, he is the author of three books, *Mr Nice*, *The Howard Marks Book Of Dope Stories,* and *Señor Nice*.

Mashed Main Courses

In the wild, if left alone, cannabis grows successfully almost anywhere, but particularly in Afghanistan and Morocco, where the heat can cause plants to grow an impressive 20 feet high! Put that in your pipe and smoke it. Better yet, put it into one of these recipes.

Here's the main event: the entrées. These can be served with just an appetizer or just a dessert, or on their own, depending on the robustness of the guests and host! Take your pick from eight mouthwatering marvels, sourced from the far corners of the world. There's a stew from Ireland, curry from India, pasta from Italy, falafels from Iran, and more besides. Like cannabis, good quality cooking knows no boundaries or national borders.

Puffed-Up Pizza

The perfect complement to the Ganja Garlic Bread (*see page 32*), this pot-based pizza is perfect for a night in with a few friends, some brews, and an all-night video game session. It's sure to make those high scores mean so much more!

YOU WILL NEED

Dough Base

13oz/400g/3$\frac{1}{2}$ cups all-purpose flour, plus
    extra for dredging

1oz/28g yeast

1 tbsp granulated sugar

1 cup/8fl oz/250ml warm water

1 tsp salt

2 tbsp melted cannabis ghee*

*see pages 28–29 for specific requirements

Topping

1 large onion, sliced

1 red bell pepper

4–5 tbsp melted cannabis ghee*

6oz/175g mushrooms, sliced

1–2 cans chopped tomatoes

1–2 tsp fresh or dried oregano

12 pitted olives, chopped

2 cups/8oz/250g grated cheese

*see pages 28–29 for specific requirements

MAKES 2 PIZZAS

HOW TO PREPARE

1 To make the base, the flour, yeast, and sugar are sifted into a large mixing bowl.

2 The water is added so it can be kneaded into a dough, then covered with a cloth and left in a warm place to rise for 30 minutes.

3 The salt and melted ghee are added, and then the dough is kneaded into a ball, dredged with flour, and set aside.

4 For the topping, the onion and red bell pepper are gently sautéed in the ghee for a few minutes, then the mushrooms. A few more minutes of sautéeing helps things along.

5 The tomatoes and oregano are in next, and simmered until cooked through and reduced down.

6 The dough is rolled out into two circles so the topping can be spread evenly over each one.

7 Chopped olives and grated cheese are sprinkled over the top and the pizzas are either broiled or baked in a piping hot oven for 10–15 minutes at 400°F/200°C.

ALTERNATIVE

Sprinkling over some quality dried bud, instead of putting oregano into the topping, gives a real blast of bhang.

Pot Pesto & 'Erb Pasta

Individually these two accompaniments work well, but put them both together and they are the deadliest pair since nitro met glycerin! Watch the culinary sparks fly!

YOU WILL NEED

Pot Pesto

$2^2/_3$ tsp prime cannabis bud, finely
  chopped with the stalks and
  seeds removed*

large bunch of fresh basil

$1/_3$ cup pine nuts or walnuts

1 cup/60g fresh parsley, chopped

2 garlic cloves

juice of 1 small lemon

$1/_3$ cup/90ml olive oil

filtered water (optional)

*see pages 28–29 for specific requirements

'Erb Pasta

scant 1 cup/4oz/115g all-purpose white
  flour, plus extra for dusting

scant 1 cup/4oz/115g semolina flour

2 large eggs

2 tsp olive oil

handful of finely chopped fresh or dried
  cannabis leaves*

$1/_2$ tsp salt

*see pages 28–29 for specific requirements

SERVES 2–4

HOW TO PREPARE

PESTO

1 All but the oil is thrown into a blender and given a whirl.

2 Then the olive oil is drizzled in, and maybe some water, until the consistency is right.

PASTA

1 The flours are sifted into a heap on a clean counter, or into a bowl.

2 A well is made in the center to which the other ingredients are added.

3 The egg mixture in the well can be mixed up with fingertips and then flour is incorporated from around the edges bit by bit until a crumbly dough has formed.

4 A few drops of water mean it can be kneaded into a stiff paste.

5 More kneading, on a floured counter, should follow until the dough has a smooth, elastic consistency. It is then covered in plastic wrap and set aside for an hour.

6 The dough is rolled out on a floured counter, being turned round occasionally, until paper thin. It can be made into whatever shape the cook chooses. This last stage is made much simpler if there's a pasta machine in the kitchen!

7 The pasta is boiled for 3–4 minutes, drained, and served with the pesto on top.

Roasted, Wasted Vegetables

This delicious veggie roast is a perennial favorite and perfect for a chilled-out Sunday lunch with friends. So many nutritious vegetables are bound to be good for you, too. Serve with mounds of brown rice.

YOU WILL NEED

6 potatoes, roughly chopped

1–1 1/2 cups/230–350g cannabis ghee*

4 carrots, chopped

4 parsnips or something similar, chopped

2 bell peppers (1 green, 1 red), chopped

2 zucchini, chopped

1 squash, chopped

6 whole garlic cloves
   (with skins still on them)

pinch of coriander seeds, crushed

pinch of oregano

fresh sea salt and freshly ground
   black pepper

*see pages 28–29 for specific requirements

SERVES 4–6

HOW TO PREPARE

1 The potatoes are par-boiled for 10 minutes, until they start to go soft on the outside.

2 Once drained, the potatoes are shaken in the pan to fluff them up, then set aside.

3 The fat is melted in a large roasting pan and all the chopped vegetables can go in when it starts to spit.

4 The vegetables are roasted for about an hour at 250°F/120°C, until they turn golden. Twenty minutes in, the salt, pepper, oregano, coriander seeds, and garlic are added, to taste. Some people add 1 teaspoon of ground cannabis leaf at this stage, for a slightly stronger dish.

Charas Curry

From the land of Buddha and Shiva—both enlightened cannabis connoisseurs—comes a curry like no other. Charas, the Indian name for that most sacred of herbs, cheers up this beefy beauty, but it can be equally tasty served up with chicken, or vegetables for Hindu and Buddhist guests.

YOU WILL NEED

1–2 fresh red chiles
2 tsp ground coriander
2 tsp ground turmeric
1 tsp mustard seeds
$\frac{1}{2}$ tsp ground ginger
$\frac{1}{4}$ tsp ground pepper
$1\frac{1}{4}$ cups/300ml coconut milk
2oz/55g cannabis ghee*
2 onions, sliced
3 garlic cloves
1lb 9oz/700g lean chuck steak,
   cut into cubes
1 cup/250ml beef stock
1 tbsp lemon juice
large handful of fresh cilantro
salt and pepper

*see pages 28–29 for specific requirements

SERVES 4–6

HOW TO PREPARE

1 The onions and garlic need sautéeing in the ghee in a pan until golden brown, then the spice paste can go in, and frying continues for another 2 minutes.

2 The chiles are chopped and put in a bowl with all the spices. The addition of a little coconut milk helps it come together into a smooth paste.

3 The chopped beef and stock are added, and the pan is brought to a boil.

4 The stew gets left to simmer on a low heat for 1 hour.

5 The rest of the coconut milk and the lemon juice are added, and the whole lot gets brought to a boil before serving. Salt and pepper can be added to taste.

6 It is best served with tons of fresh cilantro as a garnish, or mixed into rice. Poppadums and nan bread are essential! If your guests prefer a milder touch, a side order of natural yogurt can be served instead to cool the curry down.

I Arrest Stew
(in the name of the law)

This is one of those phrases no one ever wants to hear, but it's a dish that everyone will want to eat! Essentially it's a good, hearty, traditional Irish stew, but with that little extra special ingredient. A wicked weed winter warmer!

YOU WILL NEED

2½–3lb/1.35kg lamb chops

8 onions

8 carrots

1 tbsp cannabutter*

3-3½ cups/750–900ml stock
   (lamb, ideally)

8 potatoes

sprig of fresh thyme

cornstarch

1 tbsp chopped fresh parsley

1 tbsp chopped fresh chives

salt and pepper

*see pages 28–29 for specific requirements

SERVES 6–8

HOW TO PREPARE

1 The chops are cut in half and any excess fat is removed.

2 The onions and carrots need peeling, and cutting into large chunks.

3 The excess fat from the meat is melted in a pan and the meat tossed in it until slightly brown.

4 The meat is transferred to a casserole dish, then the onions and carrots are quickly tossed in the cannabutter.

5 The veg and remaining butter are chucked into the casserole dish and seasoned with pepper and salt. The lamb stock is poured into the casserole.

6 The potatoes are peeled and stuck on top of the casserole, so they steam while the stew cooks. A sprig of thyme is added, then the casserole is brought to boil on top of the stove, covered with a butter wrapper or paper lid, and the lid of the pan. It can be placed in the oven (preheated to 350°F/180°C) or allowed to simmer on low heat until cooked, which should take about an hour and a half.

7 When the stew is cooked, the cooking liquid is poured off and reheated in another pan. It can be thickened by whisking in a little cornstarch and more cannabutter (for the adventurous only!). With the chopped herbs added, it can be poured over the meat and vegetables.

8 The stew needs taking back up to boiling point before serving.

Chile Bean Pot

This isn't the sort of chile you buy in U.S. stores, but a real home-down, Tex-Mex, four-alarm fire of a meal! Delectable and dangerous in equal measure. Mexico is not only the home of chile, but also that classic seventies strain of weed, Acapulco Gold.

YOU WILL NEED

2lb/1kg pinto beans
1lb/500g bacon, chopped
2 cups/500ml red wine
4 tbsp chile powder
2 garlic cloves
$2^2/_3$ tsp chopped grass*
$1/_2$ cup/50g mushroom, chopped
beef or vegetable stock cube, optional
salt and pepper
rice or nachos, and sour cream, to serve
*see pages 28–29 for specific requirements

SERVES 10

HOW TO PREPARE

1 All the ingredients go in a big pot with enough water or stock to cover.

2 It's brought to a boil and then left to simmer for about an hour, or until it tastes right. Salt and pepper can be added to taste.

3 This dish is great served with rice or nachos, and a spot of cooling sour cream.

Seriously Sprouted Hemp Seed Falafels

This traditional Middle Eastern "fast food" is healthier than a burger and more tasty than deep-fried chicken. This certainly won't get you high but it tastes so good that you won't care! The perfect snack for those munchie moments when all the potato chips, brownies, and cookies have been eaten.

YOU WILL NEED

1 cup/250g sprouted hemp seeds*

1 onion, chopped

2 garlic cloves

1 tsp ground cumin

2 cups/400g red lentils

2½ cups/600ml vegetable stock

3 cups/720g chickpeas

handful of fresh cilantro

1 cup/250g sesame seeds

salt and pepper

olive oil, for sautéeing

pitas, to serve

*see pages 28–29 for specific requirements

MAKES 15–20

HOW TO PREPARE

1 The hemp seeds are soaked overnight and then left on a flat tray or a sprouter—where they need rinsing and draining several times a day—until they start to germinate.

2 The onion and garlic are sautéed in olive oil (or some cannabutter), and the cumin goes in when the onions start to turn brown. A good mix with a wooden spoon is recommended.

3 The red lentils and vegetable stock are put in a pan and simmered gently for about 15 minutes, until all the stock is absorbed and the lentils are tender.

4 In a blender, the chickpeas are puréed and added to the red lentils, along with the sprouted hemp seeds and cilantro. Seasoning is added according to taste.

5 The mix is left to stand for 20 minutes in a cool place so the moisture is absorbed, then worked into small patties.

6 The patties are rolled in sesame seeds and pan-fried until golden brown. Traditionally they are served in pitas with salad, mayonnaise, hummus, or sesame seed paste.

BRYAN TALBOT'S

Far-Out Spag

A quick, delicious, and fresh-tasting entrée by Bryan Talbot for his character Chester P. Hackenbush—C.P. loves this with tons of black pepper and 15 cloves of garlic!

YOU WILL NEED

6oz/175g long spaghetti

4 tbsp extra virgin olive oil

10 garlic cloves (adjust to taste)

1lb/500g tomatoes, chopped

Splash of dry white wine

1 tbsp dried, crumbled grass*

$\frac{1}{2}$ cup/35g fresh basil leaves

$\frac{1}{2}$ small can pitted black olives (drained!)

Fresh ground black pepper and vegetable
   bouillon or salt

1oz/28g whole arugula leaves

4oz/115g local cheese (grated)

*see pages 28–29 for specific requirements

SERVES 2–4

HOW TO PREPARE

1 A pan of water is brought to a boil and then the spaghetti is added and left to cook, stirring occasionally, for about 8–10 minutes, depending on how *al dente* you like it.

2 The olive oil is heated in a large pan and the garlic is gently sautéed for a minute, being careful not to let it burn. The heat is turned up and the tomatoes, wine, grass, basil, olives, black pepper, and bouillon, are added and stirred well. The heat is then turned down and the pan left to simmer, keeping it moist and stirring occasionally until the ingredients are slightly reduced and the spaghetti is done.

3 The spaghetti is drained and served in two large pasta bowls. Then the sauce is poured over, the arugula is added and the cheese is sprinkled on the top. The cheese melts as you eat.

BRYAN TALBOT

Starting in underground comics such as *Brainstorm*, Bryan has worked in the area of adult comics, graphic novels, and SF illustration for over 25 years. He is the creator of cult counterculture tokin' hero, Chester P. Hackenbush as well as *The Adventures of Luther Arkwright*, *Heart of Empire,* and *The Tale of One Bad Rat*.

Doped-Out Desserts

When most people think of cannabis cooking they associate it with sweet, baked food. Classic hash brownies, cookies, and "space" cakes are all firm favorites in the gallery of grass gastronomy. There's just something magical in the munchies that brings out the sweet tooth in everyone.

Any guest that has made it through the stoned starters and mashed main courses deserves a medal, or at least a long quiet lie down. But we've still got the dessert menu to get through. This is the sucker punch, with recipes so tempting even the fullest diner will find it difficult to "Just Say No."

Even better, most of the recipes can be produced well in advance (probably a very good idea, if the host has also been enjoying the meal!) and are really quite simple to make. The cannabis kick in these desserts varies, but—as with all the recipes—they can always be boosted or toned down to suit individual preference. All the classics are here, plus a few new spins on old favorites. And of course, they don't need to be served exclusively as desserts. These dishes can be enjoyed any time of the day or night as a snack with a lovely fresh cup of tea or coffee.

Crash Brownies

Brownies have been a treasured recipe in the armory of cannabis cuisine ever since Alice B. Toklas included one in her classic 1954 cookbook. For the perfect finish to that special dinner these particular honey-flavored "Crash Brownies" have a rich, complex flavor and velvety texture guaranteed to please the most discerning guest.

YOU WILL NEED

6oz/175g unsweetened chocolate

6oz/175g cannabutter*

2 cups/700g honey

4 eggs

1 tsp salt

1 tbsp vanilla extract

4 cups/560g all-purpose flour

*see pages 28–29 for specific requirements

MAKES 10–15

HOW TO PREPARE

1 The chocolate needs melting in a double-boiler pan, then the cannabutter and honey are mixed in.

2 Next in, the eggs, swiftly followed by the salt, vanilla, and flour.

3 Now it's poured into a greased square oven pan (9 x 12in/23 x 30cm) and baked for 35 minutes at 375°F/190°C.

4 The brownies are allowed to cool and set for 1 hour before cutting. The trick is not to overcook them or they dry out. But if they are taken out too early, they end up a gooey mess!

5 Brownies are usually cut into 2-in/5-cm squares, and can be frozen or served with coffee or a refreshing tea.

ALTERNATIVE

Things can be pepped up a bit by adding 3 tablespoons of a quality whiskey bourbon like Jack Daniels, Wild Turkey, Crown Royal, or even a cognac to enrich the flavor. Also, 1 cup of sliced cherries and 2 tablespoons of brandy can be added, or 2 tablespoons of instant coffee crystals dissolved in 1 tablespoon of hot water.

Fudge Freak-Out

Fudge always goes down well and this delightful concoction makes an extra special birthday or Christmas present for that singular stoner. Allegedly, this unctuous confection was created on February 14, 1886 (Valentine's Day), when a batch of caramels was bungled—hence the name "fudge."

YOU WILL NEED

4oz/115g fresh leaves (cannaflour)*

4oz/115g butter

1 cup/250ml condensed milk

⅓ cup/90ml milk

2 cups/14oz/425g superfine sugar

1 tsp vanilla extract

*see pages 28–29 for specific requirements

MAKES 10

HOW TO PREPARE

1 All your leaf matter is ground up in a coffee grinder.

2 The butter is melted in a pan on low heat and then the cannaflour is tossed in and simmered for an hour or two.

3 The milks, sugar, and vanilla are thrown into the pan at this point and the mixture is stirred over low heat until the sugar has completely dissolved.

4 The heat is turned up to bring things to a boil. Boiling continues until the mixture reaches 250°F/120°C.

5 With the pan off the heat, the mixture needs stirring vigorously for about 4 minutes.

6 It can now be poured on to a greased tray and, when the fudge has cooled and almost set, cut into 30 equal squares.

7 Once cool, the fudge can be wrapped in waxed paper and stored in an airtight container.

SWEET HIGH

Two pieces of fudge is the equivalent of one good joint, but it will take anything from an hour up to kick in.

ALTERNATIVE

The butter and cannaflour can be replaced with cannabutter, or the milk with cannamilk. If you want to sleep for a month, go with all three! This fudge also tastes delicious with raisins or hazelnuts mixed in.

Ganja Goo-Balls

A perennial favorite among stoner connoisseurs, this candy goes down well after dinner, but is just as enjoyable with coffee and muffins on the lawn. The ideal way to idle away a lazy summer's day!

YOU WILL NEED

1 cup/250g cannabutter*, melted

3 cups/225g oats

1 cup/250g peanut butter (smooth or chunky!)

3 tbsp honey

2 tbsp ground cinnamon

1–2 tbsp cocoa powder

*see pages 28–29 for specific requirements

MAKES 15

HOW TO PREPARE

1 All the ingredients are thrown into one large bowl and stirred until the stirrer's arm aches and it's all mixed in.

2 The bowl is popped into the freezer for 10–20 minutes.

3 The mixture is molded into individual balls, and dropped on to waxed paper to set.

ALTERNATIVE

Chopped walnuts, raisins, corn flakes, or Rice Krispies can be added as an experiment! If the result is too gooey, more oats can be added. If it's too dry, more peanut butter or honey can be added. Really, you can try anything—it just comes down to personal taste.

Chilled-Out Banana Bob's Ice-Cream

One of the best foods to enjoy while stoned is ice-cream. The sensation of scrumptious flavors slowly melting in the mouth is hard to beat. As the ice-cream warms up so does the THC and the combined effect is bliss. Be warned, it can be hard to stop eating this manna from hemp heaven!

YOU WILL NEED

scant 2¹/₂ cups/575ml light cream

2 tbsp/25g cannabutter*

¹/₃ cup/75g light brown sugar

15oz/450g bananas

5 tbsp honey

¹/₄ cup/40g chopped hazelnuts
    or pistachios

*see pages 28–29 for specific requirements

SERVES 6

HOW TO PREPARE

1 The cream is slowly heated in a pan until almost boiling. In another pan the cannabutter is melted with the sugar. The hot cream is then whisked in with the butter.

2 The bananas are peeled and mashed with a fork. The cream, honey, and nuts are added and mixed in well. The mixture is poured into a chilled freezerproof container, covered, and frozen for a few hours until the mixture is a mushy consistency. The mixture is scooped into a chilled bowl and beaten until smooth.

3 The mixture is returned to the container, covered, and frozen until ready to serve. The ice-cream is transferred to the refrigerator 30 minutes before serving to soften and can be served with cookies and wafers.

STAY CHILLED

The easiest way to make this is to throw all the ingredients into an ice-cream maker.

Little Nibbly Bits

In the 13th century, Sufis would create a form of "chewing gum" from cannabis leaves and hemp seeds mixed with sesame paste and sugar. In 2006, a bunch of students in Maryland, USA, placed small amounts of cannabis inside hollowed-out gumballs and called them "Greenades." For those with a bit more culinary flair this classic 1969 recipe from Mary Jane Superweed's *Super Candy* is a good place to start.

YOU WILL NEED

1lb/500g roasted cashew butter

1 tbsp cannabutter*

3–4 tsp honey

2 cups/186g shredded/desiccated coconut

$^{1}/_{2}$ cup/60g ground almond meal

$^{3}/_{4}$ cup/125g dried currants

*see pages 28–29 for specific requirements

MAKES 20

HOW TO PREPARE

1   The butters and honey are creamed together in a bowl.

2   On a flat tray, the coconut and almond meal are mixed together.

3   The honeyed butter ball is rolled and kneaded into the coconut/almond mix. As the cashew picks up the coconut it becomes less tacky. When both are blended, the currants are spread on the tray.

4   The currants are rolled and kneaded into the dough. Anyone who wants a tasty nibbly bit can now feel free to break a bit off.

ALTERNATIVE

Crunchy peanut butter can be used instead of cashew butter, but the flavor will be stronger.

Mad-For-It Moroccan Majoun

Hashish (processed cannabis) makes up 0.57 percent of Morocco's Gross Domestic Product (GDP) and 10 percent of the country's land is dedicated to growing it. That's a lot of grass! Majoun is a traditional Moroccan way of eating cannabis. There are several ways of making it, and consistencies vary from a small date-like candy to a runnier jelly.

YOU WILL NEED

1½ tsp cleaned, ground cannabis*
1 cup/180g chopped dates
½ cup/145g chopped raisins
½ cup/75g ground walnuts
½ cup/75g ground almonds
1 tsp ground nutmeg
1 tsp ground anise
1 tsp ground ginger
1 cup/350g honey
¼ cup/50ml water
2 tbsp melted butter or ghee
*see pages 28–29 for specific requirements

MAKES 1 LARGE POT

HOW TO PREPARE

1 In a dry skillet, the cannabis is toasted over very low heat until it begins to release an aroma.

2 The dried fruit, walnuts, almonds, spices, honey, and water is mixed in, and it's all heated through to soften the ingredients.

3 Transfer takes place to a heavy bowl so it can be mashed until well blended.

4 The ghee butter goes in last and is stirred in thoroughly. It can be spooned into a jar and stored in the refrigerator. It is delicious served on crackers, or eaten by the spoonful or fingerful. If the butter isn't added at the end, it can be shaped into candies and served individually.

Bingo Bongo Banana Bread

This is one of the best cannabis desserts around. The only problem with it is that it tastes so good, it's hard to stop eating it! A big, bad blast of banana and bhang, guaranteed to benevolently bash anyone, anytime.

YOU WILL NEED

$^1/_2$ cup/125g nonhydrogenated shortening (it's healthier!)

1 cup/200g superfine sugar

2 eggs, beaten

1 cup/225g mashed bananas

1 tsp lemon juice

2 cups/300g sifted all-purpose flour

$^1/_2$ tsp salt

3 tsp baking powder

3 tsp grass, chopped*

1 cup/150g chopped nuts

*see pages 28–29 for specific requirements

MAKES 1 LOAF

HOW TO PREPARE

1 The shortening and sugar are mixed together, and then in go the eggs.

2 The bananas should be mixed separately with the lemon juice and then added to the mix.

3 The flour, salt, and baking powder are sifted together, then mixed with the remaining ingredients.

4 This is baked in a preheated oven at 375°F/190°C for 1$^1/_4$ hours. Allow to cool before eating.

Multi-Choc Chip Koma Kookies

Here's one for all the chocolate fiends out there. Not one, not two, but three types of chocolate chip, all in one crazy cookie! Quick and easy, these shouldn't take more than an hour to make. These are delicious with tea, coffee, and a good gossip.

YOU WILL NEED

1 cup/250g cannabutter*

²/₃ cup/125g sugar

²/₃ cup/125g brown granulated sugar

1 large egg

1 tsp vanilla extract

2 cups/280g all-purpose flour

¹/₂ tsp baking soda

¹/₂ tsp salt

1 small milk chocolate bar/chips

1 small dark chocolate bar/chips

1 small white chocolate bar/chips

*see pages 28–29 for specific requirements

MAKES 12 LARGE COOKIES

HOW TO PREPARE

1 The butter and the sugars are creamed together in a bowl.

2 The egg is beaten in and the vanilla added.

3 The flour, baking soda, and salt are sifted into the creamed mixture and folded in.

4 The chocolate bars can be broken into the dough or the chips sprinkled in. Then the chocolate needs folding into the mix.

5 The dough is placed on a greased baking sheet. Recommended baking time is 8–10 minutes in a preheated oven at 375°F/190°C.

6 The baked dough can be cut into pieces with a knife or cookie cutter.

ALTERNATIVE

This basic cookie recipe can be adapted in all sorts of ways, such as replacing the chocolate for peanut butter and real peanuts, or dropping in raisins and other dried fruit.

Freaky Fridge Cake

Here's a cake that takes no time at all if you use a microwave. If you use a conventional oven, just whack the temperature up as far as it will go and the melting process should take about 10 minutes. This instant cake is the type that can be found in many cafés, snack bars, and delis and requires very little effort.

YOU WILL NEED

4oz/125g bittersweet chocolate

5oz/150g cannabutter*

2 tbsp corn syrup

8oz/250g cookies, broken

3oz/85g mixed chopped nuts
   (cashews and brazil nuts are best)

*see pages 28–29 for specific requirements

SERVES 8–16

HOW TO PREPARE

1 The chocolate is broken into small pieces and put it in an ovenproof bowl with the butter and syrup. This goes into a microwave on full power for 4 minutes.

2 The cookies and nuts are now ready to go in, and then it can all be scooped into a well-greased shallow pan.

3 The mixture goes into the refrigerator (or freezer, if impatient!) and is allowed to cool for 2 hours before serving.

Pot Pancakes with Funky Fruit

Pancakes are always good, and not just on Mardi Gras. They are a nice light sign-off after a heavy meal. Add deliciously healthy fresh fruit and it's a recipe for success every time. Of course ice-cream or whipped cream and maple syrup make a great recipe even better!

YOU WILL NEED

¼ cup/35g all-purpose flour

2 tbsp baking powder

2 tsp brown sugar

pinch of ground cinnamon

½ tsp salt

2 tbsp vegetable or sunflower oil

½ cup/125ml water

¼ cup/50ml cannamilk (see page 92)*

1 banana

handful of strawberries

handful of blueberries

butter, for sautéeing

1 tsp brown sugar

*see pages 28–29 for specific requirements

MAKES 6–8

HOW TO PREPARE

1 To make the pancake batter, the flour, baking powder, sugar, cinnamon, and salt are sifted into a large bowl and mixed thoroughly.

2 The oil, water, and cannamilk are mixed in a separate bowl.

3 The mixtures now get combined. Minimal stirring is required, and the batter should be slightly lumpy, as this makes the pancakes light and fluffy.

4 The fruit is chopped and lightly sautéed in butter and a little brown sugar in a separate skillet over low heat.

5 A little oil is heated in another skillet and the batter is poured in, while the pan is turned to ensure even coverage.

6 The pancakes are flipped when the surface bubbles. When cooked on both sides they are removed from the heat and put on a warmed plate.

7 The cooked fruit can be placed in the pancake and wrapped up. Pancakes can be decorated with strained plain yogurt, heavy cream, grated chocolate, or ice-cream.

ALTERNATIVE

Cannabutter can be used to cook the fruit in, or it can be flambéed in a cannabis brandy tincture (see page 27), for that extra kick that will leave you languishing throughout Lent!

ED ROSENTHAL'S

Greenies

This recipe is made with marijuana leaf flour (cannaflour), because it takes time to concoct an extract. It's the old "I want to get high now, damn it" syndrome. Just like the girl scouts, it pays to be prepared.

YOU WILL NEED

1 cup/8fl oz/250ml melted butter or oil

1 cup//8fl oz/250ml milk or soy milk

1 medium egg

2 oz/50g cannaflour*

1 cup/200g superfine sugar

1 tsp orange extract (optional)

1 tsp nutmeg, grated (optional)

1 tsp baking powder

2 cups/16oz/450g wheat flour

*see pages 28–29 for specific requirements

MAKES 24 GREENIES

ED ROSENTHAL

Ed Rosenthal is a worldwide authority on marijuana, a best-selling author, and a member of the International Cannabinoid Research Society.

HOW TO PREPARE

1   The butter, milk, egg, and marijuana flour are beaten together for 5 minutes, then the sugar, orange extract, and nutmeg are mixed in.

2   The baking powder and wheat flour are folded into the batter and then beaten with a mixer until thoroughly blended.

3   The batter is spooned on to a greased cookie sheet by the tablespoon and baked in the oven, preheated at 300°F/150°C for 25–30 minutes.

CANNAFLOUR

1   To make a flour from marijuana leaf, twigs or other woody debris are removed.

2   The leaves are processed in a food processor or other grinding machine until they are ground to a powder. For best results grind them down even further in a coffee mill. The powder is then sifted to remove any remaining debris and stored in a refrigerator or freezer.

3   During processing, a white dust may be kicked up, especially if the grass is very dry. This activates the capitate glands, the potent part of marijuana. Let the dust settle before opening the processor, and collect any dust that may escape.

Bombed-Out Beverages & Crazy Cocktails

You know by now that cannabis cooking isn't limited to cookies or hippy-style stews. It's not even limited to food. There are dozens, if not hundreds, of ways that cheeky little plant can be used in drinks, from winter warmers to cool summer cocktails. At the time of writing, a new ice tea is being launched in the U.K. called C-Ice, grown from Swiss hemp using the blossom syrup and extract of hemp bloom. It has all the psychoactive ingredients removed and is being marketed as a health drink, with good reason.

But tea is just the tip of the iceberg. Cannabis can be fermented, like any plant, and turned into beer and wine—although this does tend to remove, or at least reduce, the THC levels. Cannabis also breaks down very well in alcohol, and making a ready-to-use tincture (*see page 27*) is a convenient way of adding some THC to a favorite tipple. A cannabis cooking brandy can be used in treats like Pot Pancakes with Funky Fruit (*see page 86*). For other mouthwatering suggestions, take a look through the recipes in this chapter.

Holy Cow Hot Chocolate

This is a festival favorite, just what you need when you've been wandering around a field for hours in the chilly night air. Delicious and irresistible, it'll warm up the coldest raver and chill out the maddest party animal! It takes about an hour to kick in and is really, really relaxed and mellow.

YOU WILL NEED

1 cup/250ml milk

5 tbsp granulated sugar

1 cup/250ml light cream

pinch of ground cinnamon

$\frac{1}{2}$ tsp vanilla extract

$\frac{1}{8}$oz/4g cannabis*, finely chopped

5oz/150g unsweetened or plain chocolate

1 chocolate bar, whipped cream and/or
   baby marshmallows, to decorate

*see pages 28–29 for specific requirements

MAKES 2 CUPS or 1 BIG ONE

HOW TO PREPARE

1   The milk and sugar are combined in a pan over medium heat. Once the sugar has dissolved, all the other ingredients can be added, apart from the chocolate.

2   After boiling, it simmers for about 1 hour, and then is filtered through a permanent coffee filter (a paper one would be too fine). The fats in the milk release the THC, making cannamilk.

3   The cannamilk is poured back into the pan so the chocolate can be added. With the heat off, it can be stirred until the chocolate has melted.

4   The drink is usually served in a mug, or mugs, topped with thick, whipped cream. Fans grate their favorite chocolate bar over the top or use it as an edible swizzle stick—or keep it classic and break open a package of marshmallows.

Lassi Come Home

Lassis and bhangs (yogurt or milk-based drinks) are standard fare in India, but many an unwary traveler has discovered that appearances can be deceptive. This baby looks harmless, but beneath its benevolent façade lurks the mother of all big bhangs!

YOU WILL NEED

large handful of bhang
    (fresh cannabis* leaves and bud)
granulated sugar, to taste
³/₄oz/25g blanched almonds
1¹/₂oz/50g Gulkand (rose petal jam)
cardamom, to taste
8 cups/2 liters milk
1 cup/250ml Malai (thickened milk)
    or heavy cream
black pepper, to garnish

*see pages 28–29 for specific requirements

MAKES 2

HOW TO PREPARE

1 The leaves are ground with a little black pepper using a mortar and pestle.

2 Some sugar, the almonds, Gulkand, and cardamom are added next, and ground into a paste. Some alternative ingredients worth trying are pistachios, raisins, or mangoes.

3 The milk is mixed in, and then the concoction is strained over a pail. The Malai, or cream, can be added and then it goes in the refrigerator.

4 A pinch of black pepper is sprinkled over the top as a garnish. Serving this in a communal goblet, chalice, or similar would be appropriate, though not essential. Perfect for summer picnics, or barbecues where all the food gets burned! Once they've had some of this, guests won't care!

SHIVA'S DRINK

Before drinking, especially from a communal vessel, the first taste is offered to Shiva, symbolized by a few drops on the pestle.

Coffee & Tea

Let's give the two most popular drinks in the world (after water) a sinsemilla spin.

YOU WILL NEED

Coffee

1 freshly brewed pot of good coffee
(Java's good but any freshly ground
Arabica bean will do)

4 tsp finely-powdered straight Arabian
mocha

2 pinches of ground cinnamon

2 pinches of ground nutmeg

generous pinch of pulverized hashish*

1 tsp honey, per cup, to taste

Tea

1 cup/250ml mint or green tea (must
be hot)

2 tbsp cannabutter*

milk and sugar to taste (optional, but
recommended)

*see pages 28–29 for specific requirements

MAKES 2 CUPS

HOW TO PREPARE
COFFEE

Recent studies have revealed that four cups of "hot joe" a day can reduce the risk of cirrhosis of the liver by 80 percent. Add to this the benefits of cannabis and it's a winner every time, especially after a heavy night out. This recipe is reminiscent of dawamesk, a strong Arabic coffee and a favorite tipple at Club des Haschichins (see page 15). Treat with respect!

1 The fresh coffee is poured into a Turkish coffee pot containing all the other ingredients, save the honey.

2 The coffee gets heated on a low flame, until it threatens to bubble over, and then is removed quickly from the heat.

3 The coffee is served in small espresso cups with a spoon each, and the honey mixed in. The powdered mocha, honey, and other residues can then be eaten like candy from the bottom with the spoon.

CHARAS CHA

There's more than one way to brew a good cup of cha (the Chinese word for tea) with charas (the Indian word for cannabis). The easiest way to make cannabis tea is to pour boiling water over $1/3$ teaspoon of powdered cannabis and to let it infuse for an hour and a half. Then reheat and melt in 1 teaspoon of butter. But the following recipe can give a better high:

1 Tea is simply made in the usual way, then the butter is stirred in so it melts.

2 Milk and sugar are added according to taste and that's it. Niiiccee!

All these drinks go great with Ed Rosenthal's Greenies (see page 88).

Completely Château-ed

Making hemp wine involves a lot of work but the end result is worth it. You can buy the equipment and get all the advice you need from a store that caters to home winemakers.

EQUIPMENT

50-pint/30-liter food-grade plastic
    container
40-pint/23-liter glass or plastic
    food-grade carboy
airlock and rubber bung (for carboy)
hydrometer
long, narrow tube or jar
dairy thermometer
5-ft/1.5-m piece of food-grade plastic tubing
1 long spoon
wine thief (to remove the developing
    wine from the carboy)
sodium metabisulfite for sanitizing
30 bottles and 30 corks

INGREDIENTS

fresh cannabis* buds soaked in 40 pints/
    23 liters of good quality, filtered
    warm water
white wine yeast
9–11lb/4–5kg corn sugar
1 tsp gelatin powder
*see pages 28–29 for specific requirements

MAKES 30 BOTTLES

HOW TO PREPARE

1 The cannabis buds and water is poured into a plastic container to take it up to 40 pints/23 liters. The temperature should be 65–75°F/18–23°C. It can be tested with a sanitized dairy thermometer and cold juice or water added to adjust the temperature.

2 Mad stirring should follow, along with the yeast and sugar.

3 The specific gravity (s.g) is checked by putting the sanitized hydrometer in the container. It should show an s.g. of about 1.010 or greater. If it's less, sugar syrup can be stirred in, then the temperature can be checked again. Next, the hydrometer is removed and the lid put on.

4 After 1–2 days the "must" should be bubbling away. Soon after, the yeast will drop to the bottom and continue to ferment.

5 After a week the carboy, bung, airlock, and plastic tubing are cleaned. The "must" is siphoned into the carboy leaving the sedimentation behind. The bung and airlock are attached, with the airlock filled halfway with water.

6 The carboy is stored in a dark, dry place. After 10 days, the s.g. is checked using a wine thief to transfer a little wine to the measuring tube. It should have an s.g. of about 0.998 or lower. Check daily until the s.g. reads the same on two consecutive days.

7 The bung and airlock are removed and the gelatin added. It needs stirring for 5 minutes. Then the bung and airlock are replaced.

8 After 14 days, the bottles and tubing can be cleaned, and the wine siphoned into bottles, and corked. The bottles sit upright for three days, then on their sides for at least a month.

Out Of It Ale

In the United States, it is legal to possess and brew sterilized hemp seeds, which can be bought easily on the Internet. These seeds contain only a trace of THC and have no psychoactive effects. But it's possible that drinking hemp beer may cause some modern drug tests to show positive, not to mention getting the drinker wasted if taken to excess!

EQUIPMENT

5-gallon/19-liter stainless steel or enamel-coated brewpot
8-gallon/30-liter food-grade plastic primary fermenter with airtight lid, airlock, and rubber stopper
plastic hose
1 large, food-grade plastic bucket with a spigot at the bottom. It must be at least as big as your primary fermenter
glass bottles

INGREDIENTS

10lb/4.5kg 2-row pale malt
1lb/500g Munich malt
1oz/25g black patent malt
1.5lb/650g mild hemp seeds (roasted)
4.5 AAU Cascade hops (90 minutes) (0.75oz/21g of 6% alpha acids)
4.5 AAU Cascade hops (45 minutes) (0.75oz/21g of 6% alpha acids)
3 AAU Cascade hops (10 minutes) (0.5oz/14g of 6% alpha acids)
4.5 AAU Cascade hops (0 minutes) (0.75oz/21g of 6% alpha acids)
1 tsp Irish moss
Wyeast 1056 (American Ale) or White Labs WLP001 (California Ale) yeast
$2/3$ cup/130g corn sugar (for priming)

MAKES ENOUGH FOR A PARTY

HOW TO PREPARE

1 The hemp seeds are roasted in an oven preheated to 450°F/230°C for 30 minutes.

2 The grains and hemp seeds are "mashed" (heated) with 3.5 gallons/13 liters of water and the corn sugar in the brewpot.

3 The mash is held at 156°F/69°C for 60 minutes.

4 Water is sprinkled—heated to 170°F/77°C—on top (aka "sparging"), to collect 5.75 gallons/22 liters of wort (the liquid left from mashing the grains and hemp).

5 Boiling should ensue for 90 minutes, with hops added at the times indicated above.

6 The Irish moss is added in the last 15 minutes. The wort is cooled and transfered to the primary fermenter. Aerate and add yeast.

7 Once left to ferment at 68°F/20°C for 10 days, transfer to the plastic bucket and bottle as required.

Green Dream Machine

Here's a cocktail that's sure to bring on nice dreams. One per person should be enough to kick-start even the dullest cocktail party and loosen those bow ties and tiaras! Just try and remember to stop at one drink or imbibers will be sorry!

YOU WILL NEED

$\frac{1}{2}$fl oz/15ml of light rum/
    cannabis tincture*

1fl oz/30ml melon liqueur

1fl oz/30ml vodka

crushed and cubed ice

lemonade

1 slice of watermelon

1 cherry

*see pages 28–29 for specific requirements

MAKES 1 LARGE GLASS

HOW TO PREPARE

1   A rum/cannabis tincture is prepared (*see page 27*).

2   The tincture, melon liqueur, vodka, and crushed ice are mixed in a cocktail shaker until frosty.

3   The mixture is then strained into a large glass globlet over cubed ice and topped with lemonade.

4   The glasses can be decorated with the melon, a cherry, and a straw.

Blasted Cow

For those that like the creaminess of a pina colada, but hate the strong coconut taste, here's a great alternative. The crème de banane overpowers the rum and so it tastes more like a banana milkshake. This cheeky little number is mellifluous in the mouth but mischievous on the mind.

YOU WILL NEED

cracked ice

1½fl oz/45ml light cream

1fl oz/30ml crème de banane

dash of grenadine

½fl oz/15ml light/white rum/cannabis*
    tincture

3 slices of banana

grated nutmeg

*see pages 28–29 for specific requirements

MAKES 2 COCKTAILS

HOW TO PREPARE

1 The ice, cream, crème de banane, grenadine, and rum tincture are thrown into a cocktail shaker and shaken vigorously for 30 secs.

2 The mix is strained into a glass, with skewered banana slices for garnish.

3 Finally, nutmeg is grated over the top.

KERPOW!

For a drink with added bang, decorate with a lit sparkler, and a small plastic cow...

Bloody Mary Jane

This twist on a classic cocktail, invented by Fernand Petiot in Paris in 1921, is perfect for the-day-after-the-night-before. As the saying goes "avoid hangovers, stay drunk!" Seriously though, this will get anyone through four to five hours, until they can face solid food again. As an alternative, use a tequila tincture to make a Bloody Maria-juana.

YOU WILL NEED

¹/₂fl oz/15ml vodka/cannabis tincture*
   (see page 27)

3 dashes Worcestershire sauce

3 drops Tabasco sauce

5fl oz/150ml tomato juice

1 tbsp lemon juice

salt and pepper

lemon twist

celery stalk

*see pages 28–29 for specific requirements

MAKES 2

HOW TO PREPARE

1 First, the tincture, sauces, and juices go into a shaker.

2 After a good shake, it is strained into a tall glass and garnished with pepper, salt, lemon twist, and a celery stalk swizzle.

ALTERNATIVE

Another simple drink with a kick like a demented mule is Green Dragon. This ethanol or vodka tincture is made with scant 1 cup/200ml of alcohol and ¹/₂oz/15g of primo bud and made the standard way. For a unique zing, 1 tablespoon of lemon or lime zest can be added. It's best served chilled in a cold glass with 3 ice cubes, 1 shot of Green Dragon, 3 shots of lemonade, and a teaspoon of honey.

SAM PEACEFULL-DAY'S

Mocha Shocker

Another classic brought to you from the wonderful Eric's Kitchen. This drink combines a traditional coffee recipe with a delicious hot, sleepy chocolate. It's very easy to make and is the perfect end to a long stoned afternoon.

YOU WILL NEED

pinch/1g of good quality hashish*

$1/4$ pt/150ml hot fresh coffee

$1/4$ pt/150ml hot fresh chocolate made with whole milk. (Made either with chocolate powder or melted chocolate—better!)

1 tsp superfine sugar

whipped cream, fine chocolate dust, or 3 chocolate coffee beans

*see pages 28–29 for specific requirements

MAKES 1 LARGE MUG

HOW TO PREPARE

1 A pinch of good hashish is warmed and ground down to a really fine powder.

2 The hot chocolate is made and poured evenly into 2 glass cups. Then, half a teaspoon of superfine sugar and half a teaspoon of the ground hashish is stirred into each cup.

3 The coffee is poured in and finished off with a squirt of whipped cream. Finally, it is sprinkled with a fine chocolate dust or 3 chocolate coffee beans.

SAM PEACEFULL-DAY

Born in London, Sam (AKA Eric!) grew up in a house of cooking, love, and laughter. It is these qualities she has carried with her on her culinary travels—she has cooked in Greek tavernas, Dutch households, and Turkish coffee bars. She regularly contributes new recipes to cannabis lifestyle magazines such as *Weed World* and *Heads*, and is the author of several highly regarded books on cooking with cannabis including: *Cannabis Café*, *Cooking with Ganja* and *Cannabis for Lunch*.

Handy Hemp

Hemp, the THC-free (or almost free) cousin of cannabis is nothing short of a miracle plant. There is seemingly nothing it can't be used for, from making paper, cloth, and even houses, to fueling cars. Whether people realize it or not, hemp is everywhere. It could be hiding in the nip and tuck of your re-sealable sandwich bag (hemp-seed-oil derivatives ensure the bags open and close smoothly), or be enhancing your listening experience with a set of state-of-the-art, high-tech "hemp horn" speakers.

In fact, this incredibly versatile and tough plant has a mind-blowing 50,000 commercial uses. The woody stem alone is currently used in 5,000 textile and 25,000 cellulose products. The stalk is used as the main ingredient in fabric, paper, paints, building materials, animal bedding, and fuel; the seeds are processed as cooking oils, fuel, lubricants, lotions, and foodstuffs; and the foliage is used in the manufacture of medicines for the mind, body, and spirit.

But for the purposes of this book, we're interested in hemp on a domestic level: let's focus on hemp as a highly nutritious foodstuff and a wonderfully effective natural beauty product.

HEMP FOODS

One of the most nutritious crops on the planet, hemp is close to being a complete food in its own right. The seeds contain high levels of healthy polyunsaturated oils, essential fatty acids (EFAs) that include the immunity-boosting omega-3, and the wonder oil GLA, which is known to reduce cholesterol and protect against PMT and arthritis.

An average hemp crop produces 55 million seeds per square hectare. The rough residue left after pressing is used in animal feed.

TOP-QUALITY PROTEIN

As well as being a great source of omega-3 fatty acids, hemp seeds are also very high in protein (25 percent), and just a handful provides the adult minimum daily protein requirement. Hemp protein includes all eight essential amino acids, which the body cannot manufacture itself, in a highly digestible form that is similar to that of blood plasma. Because the body doesn't have to work hard to make use of this protein, these healthy seeds can be an ideal solution for people who are convalescing.

Healing Hemp

So powerful is the cocktail of EFAs in hemp oil that researchers are currently working to secure hemp oil's place in the treatment of people with severely depleted immunity, such as AIDS patients.

FIBER

Hemp is a fantastic source of roughage, too, and a handful of seeds in your granola will soon sort out your system, or you can go the whole hog and stew up a hearty hemp-seed oatmeal. Seeds can also be lightly toasted and tossed in soya sauce for a tasty high-fiber snack, but be careful not to overheat them because this will destroy valuable nutrients and create carcinogens.

SPROUT YOUR OWN SEEDS

Hemp seeds can be eaten raw, but more nutrients are released if they are sprouted first. Simply soak the seeds overnight and then place them in a jar on its side with the lid off. Rinse them twice a day with fresh water and eat when the shoots are ¼–⅜in/ 5–10mm long. Soaking and sprouting breaks down the protective layers within the seeds, making them more easily digestible.

HEMP COOKING

More gourmet than gruel, hemp seeds and oil lend themselves to hundreds of tempting recipes and readymade meals. Why not enjoy a power-packed dish of sprouted hemp seeds scattered over a salad, drizzled with nutty hemp oil? Alternatively, sprouted seeds can be blended with fruit, juice, or yogurt as a hemp smoothie. Or make some green hemp milk by blending the sprouted seeds with cannabis leaves and water or soy milk. Like soy, hemp can also be texturized as a meat alternative, or it can be made into hemp seed butter, or roasted and crushed into flour for pasta, breads, and cakes.

A warning for the over-enthusiastic—for a psychotropic snack you can make use of the hemp bud, but the seeds aren't going to give you what you want. To get high you'd need to ingest the equivalent of two or three strong doses of high-fiber laxative. That kind of shit's no good to anyone!

WARNING

Hemp oil is a dish best served cold. At high temperatures, the chemical properties of the oil change and it may produce dangerous carcinogenic free-radicals.

Hemp seeds can be ground into a flour and made into bread.

HEMP PRODUCTS

Hemp can be made into almost anything, not just tasty things to eat but also clothes and products that make us look good. There's been a recent revolution in both the fashion and cosmetic industries, and our humble plant is right at the root of it.

HEMP FABRIC

Processed from the long grass fiber in the stem and expertly made, hemp produces a material as fine as linen. Until Prohibition in 1937, it was in fact a prized fabric. As Brent Moore noted in his 1905 book, *The Hemp Industry in Kentucky,* "Such is the competition to purchase hemp that it always brings the last cent that the manufacturer can afford to pay." Unfortunately, some modern hemp supplies result in fibers that are often over-lengthened, and fabric that has a tendency to shrink. Good designers pre-shrink their lines and the inventive ones include hemp rayon in their repertoire. At its best, hemp is the ultimate eco-textile: it's durable, warm, and allows the body to breathe. Yes, hemp is cool, in every sense.

The Hemp Trading Company has received massive support from stacks of hemp-friendly urban musicians, such as Morcheeba, Freq Nasty and DJ, and producer L. Double (pictured).

HEMP FASHION

Current hemp fashion is slick and hip. The Hemp Trading Company produce urban eco-wear modeled by some of the U.K.'s most influential hip-hop and drum and bass artists, including the Urban Dub Foundation, while surfer types have taken up Gekko Bay's motto, "If you smoke it you may as well wear it." These hemp designers and producers in southwest England promote and protect the lifestyle they love, "by using hemp fiber to create a more natural approach to clothing and accessories." If you're more Gaultier than grunge, take heart, even the big names of the fashion elite are embracing hemp. It's now *de rigueur* in the collections of top designers worldwide, including Katharine Hamnet.

BEAUTY PRODUCTS

Hemp is great news for your skin and hair, and is one of the best products you can use on your body. The secret of its effectiveness lies in the seeds. Pressed into oil, they form the basis of all hemp beauty products. That's because the essential fatty acids (EFAs) the seeds contain are as beneficial when applied to the skin as they are to eat. Readily absorbed into the body, they offer deep nourishment to the various layers of the skin as they go.

Hemp oil is particularly beneficial for older skin, which has a naturally lower EFA content as a result of the skin's slower metabolism. Rubbed on to mature skin, the oil compensates for the drop in the skin's own supply of essential nutrients, and helps maintain a softer, more hydrated complexion.

Hemp oil can also be used as a natural treatment for minor cuts and broken skin,

and its anti-inflammatory abilities might help to alleviate skin conditions such as atopic eczema, psoriasis, and acne.

Use the recipes on the following pages to discover how easy it is to make some of these natural beauty products at home.

The Body Shop soon caught on to the natural benefits of hemp and produced a whole range of products.

The ecological benefits of hemp mean there's more than one way of staying green!

Cosmetics

The worth of hemp seed oil is proved by a flourishing hemp beauty industry. Estimated at $5 million in 1993, the market soared to $150 million by 1999, and continues to grow. Nowadays you can choose from a wide range of hemp cosmetics, including hand creams, sunscreen, aftershave balms, and shampoos, and major retailers are responding to the market by stocking these products.

Hemp Massage Oil

One of the easiest products to make with hemp is a massage oil. Hemp is a good base oil in which to dilute essential oils before applying to the skin. Hemp oil contains a high concentration of essential linoleic fatty acids, known to repair and replenish the skin.

YOU WILL NEED

1fl oz/28ml hemp oil, as the base or carrier oil

8–10 drops of your choice of essential oil, such as lavender, geranium, or bergamot

or:

1 teaspoon of essential oil to 4fl oz/120ml of carrier oil

MAKES ENOUGH FOR SEVERAL MASSAGES

Other carrier oils offer different properties, and the carrier oil in any given product will vary according to what therapeutic benefits the product offers.

You can buy hemp oil from most health and herbal suppliers. Always choose a cold-pressed version. Hemp is a light oil, like sunflower and grapeseed oil, so is also suitable for light massage and is water-dispersible in the bath.

HOW TO PREPARE

1 The oils should be blended by shaking them together in an amber or cobalt glass bottle. Plastic bottles should be avoided, because over time the plastic will taint the oil. The jar of oil is best stored away from direct light and heat, preferably not in the bathroom where the temperature is likely to go up and down.

2 Find a friend, give them the oil, and suggest a relaxing massage.

WARNING

This oil isn't meant for drinking! Don't apply undiluted essential oils on to the skin. If you are pregnant, epileptic, have liver damage, cancer, or any other medical problem, only use oils under the guidance of a qualified aromatherapy practitioner.

Hemp Seed Soap

Hemp seed oil is one of nature's best emollients, with properties that moisturize, soften, and soothe. The high concentration of essential linoleic fatty acids in this soap will gently repair and replenish your skin, while the crushed seed casings will exfoliate it.

YOU WILL NEED

1 can (12oz/340g) 100% lye
21¹/₂fl oz/600ml distilled water
3lb 13oz/1.7kg pure coconut, olive,
    or palm oil (70%)
1lb 10oz/745g hemp oil (30%)
2fl oz/60ml essential patchouli oil
1 tbsp semicrushed hemp seeds

EQUIPMENT

goggles (optional but recommended)
medium (1³/₄–3¹/₂-pint/1–2 liter)
    heatproof bowl
large (7–10¹/₂-pint/4–6 liter) stainless
    steel pot (not aluminum or galvanized)
large plastic or wooden spoon
hand blender
shallow cardboard box lined with plastic
    trash bag (your soap mold)
rubber gloves
cooking thermometer
vinegar (for cleaning)
sharp knife (for cutting soap into bars)

MAKES 6–9 SMALL BARS

HOW TO PREPARE

1 The lye water is prepared by freezing half the distilled water into ice cubes. The ice cubes and the rest of the water are put into the bowl, then the lye is slowly stirred into the ice and water, until it is completely dissolved. The solution should be covered to keep out air and allow it to warm up to about 85°F/29°C.

2 The coconut, olive, or palm oil is melted in the large pot over medium heat until it reaches 95°F/35°C.

3 Stir the liquid fat in a clockwise direction and pour in the lye solution in a thin stream until it is all added. Mix with a hand blender until the mix cools and thickens. Do NOT stop or the mix may separate.

4 The hemp oil, the patchouli oil, and the hemp seeds are added.

5 When the "trace" from a dribble of liquid on a spoon does not sink back into the surface, the soap is ready to pour into the lined box.

6 After 3–5 hours the soap can be cut into bars with a sharp knife. The soap should be allowed to cure in the box for about a week before it is handled, and another month before using it.

WARNING

Be very careful as lye is extremely caustic and will burn the skin and eyes. Wear rubber gloves, and goggles. Wash off any splatters immediately with a solution of 10 percent vinegar and water.

Big Bhang Bath Ballistic

After a hard day's cooking in the kitchen what better way to kick back and relax with one of these fun, fizzing bath bombs. Containing hemp oil, they are good for your skin as well as your state of mind. Simply pop in your tub for a legal high.

YOU WILL NEED

1 cup/110g sodium bicarbonate

$^1/_2$ cup/60g citric acid (dry)

$^1/_2$ cup/60g cornstarch

$^1/_3$ cup/40g Epsom salts or coarse sea salt (optional)

$2^1/_2$ tbsp hemp oil

$^1/_4$ tsp bergamot oil

$^1/_4$ tsp frankincense oil

$^1/_4$ tsp lemon oil

$^1/_4$ tsp mandarin oil

$^3/_4$ tbsp water or rose water

$^1/_4$ tsp borax to emulsify

$^1/_4$ tsp green liquid food coloring

$2^1/_2$in/60mm clear plastic two-part Christmas ornament balls

MAKES 4–6

HOW TO PREPARE

1 The sodium bicarbonate, citric acid, and cornstarch are sifted together in a large bowl and mixed until well blended. Care must be taken not to inhale too much while sieving. Epsom or sea salts can be added after sifting.

2 Next, all the wet ingredients (oils, water, and food coloring) and borax are combined in a small clean jar. This is covered tightly and shaken vigorously.

3 The wet ingredients are slowly and carefully drizzled into the dry, and stirred constantly to prevent the reaction from starting, until it has the consistency of damp sand. The mixture should just start to hold together when pressed in the hand.

4 Clean, dry, and unoiled, clear plastic two-part Christmas ornament balls are used as molds. The mixture is packed hard into each mold, then some loose mixture is thrown on top and the two halves pushed hard (not twisted) together. The excess around the join can be smoothed off with the fingers.

5 After 2 minutes, the molded bomb is tapped gently once or twice against a counter, then unmolded one side at a time. The top of the mold should not be twisted, as this will split the bomb. If it splits or crumbles, the mixture can be crumbled back into the bowl and the step repeated.

6 The bombs should be left to dry for a few days to a week before using.

BUD BOMB

For that extra pizzazz mix in some dried, roughly chopped bud when you mix the dry ingredients. These will then be released when the bomb is dropped in the bath.

GLOSSARY

ANALGESIC A form of painkiller such as acetaminophen or morphine. Cannabis is still used regularly today for effective pain relief.

BHANG Indian term for the flowers and leaf of the cannabis plant, which is smoked. Also used to describe the milky drink, bhang lassi.

CANNABIDIOL, OR CBD A non-psychoactive cannabinoid that appears to reduce the euphoric effect of THC and add a sedative quality. It appears to relieve convulsion, inflammation, anxiety, and nausea.

CANNABINOIDS The active group of chemicals, which activate the body's cannabinoid receptors. There are three general types of cannabinoid: herbal, occuring uniquely in the cannabis plant; endogenous cannabinoids in humans, and other animals; and synthetic cannabinoids.

CANNABINOL, OR CBN A non-psychoactive cannabinoid formed when tetrahydrocannabinol (THC) oxidizes.

CANNABIS INDICA In 1785, French biologist Jean-Baptiste Lamarck classified this strain in India.

CANNABIS RUDERALIS An effectively non-psychoactive strain, sometimes referred to as "industrial hemp." Finally classified in 1924, by Janischevsky in Russia, although debate rages other whether this is actually a truly separate taxonomy.

CANNABIS SATIVA The first strain to be officially classified, by Carolus Linnaeus in 1753.

CANNABUTTER General term for butter that has had cannabis' THC infused throughout. A basic staple of most cannabis cooking.

CANNAMILK A form of milk with THC infused throughout, created by mixing cannabis leaves, hash, or buds, and gently heating for over an hour.

CHARAS Indian term for cannabis resin or hash, usually hand-rolled.

CHEECH AND CHONG American comedy duo Cheech Marin and Tommy Chong made nine comedy albums and eight films between 1972 and 1985, including the classic *Up In Smoke*, all of them featuring cannabis gags.

DAWAMESK A form of strong Arabic coffee mixed with large amounts of cannabis, spices, and honey. A favorite of the Club des Haschichins.

DELTA 9-TETRAHYDRACANNABINOL, OR THC The main psychoactive substance found in the cannabis plant. It was isolated by Raphael Mechoulam and Yechiel Gaoni, Israel, in 1964. In pure form it is a glassy solid when cold and becomes viscous and sticky if warmed. THC's most likely function in cannabis is to protect the plant from herbivores or pathogens.

GANJA Slang for cannabis. Often popular in Jamaica, but not as much as sinsemilla.

GHEE Ghee is a form of clarified butter very popular in Indian cooking. Because of the process used to make it, ghee does not burn as quickly as regular butter and so can be used for cooking at much higher temperatures. It also acts as an excellent carrier fat for THC.

HASH, HASHISCH, HASHEESH This is the collected trichomes of the cannabis plant, compressed and compacted into a hard to soft resin. It can vary in color from green and red hues to black.

HEMP The most common name for non-drug-related cannabis use. Hemp can be used for everything from making flour to rope and clothing, as well as biodegradable plastics.

HEMP OIL Made from crushed hemp seeds, the oil is high in essential fatty acids. Cold-pressed, unrefined hemp oil is light green, with a nutty, grassy flavor, whereas refined hemp oil is clear with little flavor or nutrients. It is widely used in body care products, lubricants, paints, and for industrial use. Antimicrobial properties make it a useful ingredient for soaps, shampoos, and detergents.

ICE-O-LATER BAG A system for extracting the fine "pollen." Iced water helps remove the trichomes in a bag and strains them out without damaging the leaf and stalk material, freeing the best quality THC. There are many versions of these bags for the processes, including Bubblebags, Shwag Bags, Kabulbaba Bags, Bubble Sacs, and the Xtractor 1000.

JOINT Slang for a cannabis cigarette.

KUSHMAN'S KUSH A strain of cannabis plant.

MAHJOUN A form of sweet or dessert with a mixture of dried fruits, nuts, and hash. Mostly found in Arabic countries such as Morocco and Egypt.

MARIJUANA Originally the Mexican term for "inebriation," marijuana was linked with the cannabis plant in the early 1930s by prohibitionists. It's the most popular term used today for the plant.

POLLEN A common, if technically incorrect, term for the sticky trichomes on the cannabis plant, which contain the highest levels of THC. Highly sought after.

ROSALES The order of flowering plants, including roses, strawberries, blackberries, raspberries, apples, pears, plums, peaches, apricots, almonds, elms, figs, hops, and of course, cannabis.

SEMIENIATKA A basic gruel/oatmeal found in Poland, Russia, and some parts of Asia, traditionally eaten around Christmas time. It is made by gently simmering hemp seed and oatmeal in water or milk, but doesn't taste too good.

SKUNK A particularly strong-smelling strain of cannabis plant, hence the name. Has some of the highest levels of THC in any strain and can cause whiteys and unconsciousness in large amounts.

SOAP BAR A particularly cheap and nasty version of hash. It is usually "watered" down with highly dangerous substances such as engine oil, mud, and feces. Always to be avoided.

"SPACE CAKE," "HASH BROWNIES," AND "CANNABIS COOKIES" These general terms are bandied about for a whole variety of cannabis recipes. They could be made out of anything, but the key ingredient is the cannabis.

THCV, OR TETRAHYDROCANNABIVARIN A psychoactive cannabinoid found in minor amounts in *Cannabis sativa*.

TINCTURE An alcoholic extract of a plant or mineral, in this case cannabis. Tinctures have a long medical history and are relatively easy to create.

TRICHOMES Fine outgrowths or appendages on plants and protists. These are of diverse structure and function, such as hairs, glandular hairs, scales, and papillae.

WEED Slang term for cannabis.

WHITE WIDOW Named for the abundance of THC crystals giving the plant a whitish tint, White Widow is a potent *indica/sativa* cross of an Indian (*indica*) and Brazilian (*sativa*) strain. It has a very fruity taste and can smell like overripe apples when drying.

RESOURCES

BOOKS

THE ALICE B. TOKLAS COOKBOOK
Alice B. Toklas, 1954
(reprinted 2001, The Lyons Press)

**BRAINSTORM: THE COMPLETE
CHESTER P. HACKENBUSH TRILOGY**
Bryan Talbot (Alchemy Press, 1982)

CANNABIS
Jonathan Green (Pavilion, 2002)

**CANNABIS CAFE: ALL YOUR FAVOURITE
RECIPES FROM ERIC'S KITCHEN**
Sam Peacefull-Day (Eric's Kitchen, 2002)

THE CANNABIS COMPANION
Steven Wishnia (Running Press, 2004)

**CANNABIS FOR LUNCH: COOKING FOR
RECREATIONAL AND THERAPEUTIC USE**
Sam Peacefull-Day (Eric's Kitchen, 1999)

**COOKING WITH GANJA: COMPLETE
GUIDE TO COOKING WITH CANNABIS**
Sam Peacefull-Day (Eric's Kitchen,
1994 and 1997)

THE EMPEROR WEARS NO CLOTHES
Jack Herer
(Quick American Archives, 1979)

THE HASHEESH EATER
Fitzhugh Ludlow
(Harper & Brothers, 1857)

THE HOWARD MARKS BOOK OF DOPE STORIES
Howard Marks (Vintage, 2001)

**MARIJUANA BEER: HOW TO MAKE
YOUR OWN HI-BREW BEER**
Ed Rosenthal (Quick American
Publishing Company, 2002)

ASK ED: MARIJUANA GOLD—TRASH TO STASH
Ed Rosenthal (Quick American
Publishing Company, 2002)

MARIJUANA GROWERS' HANDBOOK
Ed Rosenthal (Quick American
Publishing Company, 1984)

MR NICE
Howard Marks (Secker & Warburg, 1996)

**SEÑOR NICE: STRAIGHT LIFE
FROM WALES TO SOUTH AMERICA**
Howard Marks (Harvill Secker, 2006)

SPLIFFS
Nick Jones (Collins & Brown, 2003)

SPLIFFS 2
Tim Pilcher (Collins & Brown, 2004)

SPLIFFS 3
Tim Pilcher (Collins & Brown, 2005)

TALE OF ONE BAD RAT
Bryan Talbot
(Titan Books/Dark Horse Comics, 1996)

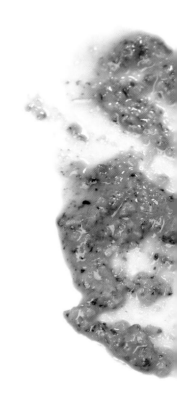

WEBSITES

ALICE IN SUNDERLAND HOME PAGE

www.bryan-talbot.com/alice/index.html

BRYAN TALBOT'S WEBSITE

www.bryan-talbot.com

ERIC'S KITCHEN WEBSITE

www.erics-kitchen.co.uk

HOWARD MARKS' WEBSITE

www.howardmarks.info

LUTHER ARKWRIGHT SITE

www.modernvikings.com/luther-arkwright

LUTHER ARKWRIGHT WEBCOMIC

www.bryan-talbot.com/lutherarkwright/

QUICK TRADING COMPANY WEBSITE

www.quicktrading.com

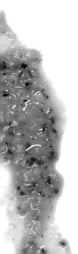

INDEX

ACKNOWLEDGMENTS

I'd like to thank Howard Marks for his introduction and recipe, but more importantly for living up to his *nom de guerre*, Mr. Nice. It is my pleasure and honor to call you a friend and scribe-in-arms—despite what you think of fellow authors! ;-)

Also a big shout out to Sam Peacefull-Day at Eric's Kitchen, Ed Rosenthal at Quicktrading.com, and Bryan Talbot. You guys really made this book and I owe you all a large round of drinks and a big fat one (or at least a heavily-laden brownie)!

I'd also like to thank the wonderful "ground crew" behind the scenes who made it all happen: Jason Hook for commissioning me; Viv Croot for nurturing the baby; Hazel Songhurst and Caroline Earle for their enduring patience, editorial input, and oversight spotting; Clare Barber, Sarah Howerd, and Andrew Perris for making the book look so good; Colin "the" Capon for all his culinary expertise, hospitality, and advice, and of course Nikki and Topsy for selling the idea in the first place. Special thanks to Julian and Raj for help with the ingredients.

Thanks also to my ex-stoner parents, whose trials and tribulations have been many, but always know that I love you both completely (a special thanks to Mom on this one, for instilling a love of cooking at an early age), Patricia, Antonia, Andrew, Kirsten, Claude, Nigel, Ian and Faye, Michael and Michelle, Phil and Sara, Randy and Renske, Rita, Michele and Dewi, Garth and Ruth, Cheeky Joe, and everyone else who suggested recipes, cooking advice, or have just been generally good, true, supportive friends over the last year.

And thanks, of course, to Sue, Megan, Oskar, Adele, Julian, and Molly for all your love, patience, and undying support. Families are what we make. Let's make ours great!

And to everyone else, keep fighting the good fight! Legalize it!

The Publishers would like to thank the following retailers for their help with props
Adamczewski, 196 High Street, Lewes. **Bright Ideas**, 38 High Street, Lewes. **Coconut**, The Needlemakers, West Street, Lewes (coconutlewes@yahoo.co.uk). **Flint**, 70 High Street, Lewes (www.flintcollection.com). **Skylark**, The Needlemakers, West Street, Lewes (skylark@fsmail.net). **Steamer Trading**, 20/21 High Street, Lewes. **Monsieur Cannelle et Compagnon**, The Needlemakers, West Street, Lewes. **Wickle Olfactory**, The Needlemakers, West Street, Lewes (www.wickle.co.uk).